How to Save the Church of England

Also by Andrew Sangster and in print with Pen & Sword Books

Pug – Churchill's Chief of Staff: The Life of General Hastings Ismay KG GCB CH DSO PC, 1887–1965 (2023)

How Hitler Evolved the Traditional Army Establishment: A Study Through Field Marshals Keitel, Paulus and Manstein (2024)

'Make Germany Great Again': How the German People Reacted to Nazism (2024)

Major Blunders of the Second World War: New Insights into Mistakes and Their Consequences (2024)

Exploring Nationalism: Identifying Its Forms, Particularly Those Which Lead to War and Mayhem (2025)

From Stalingrad to Italy – Von Senger's War: The German General Who Defied Hitler (2025)

Why Appeasement Failed: The Ignored Evidence (2025)

Oswald Mosley and A Short History of Fascism (2026)

How to Save the Church of England

The Voice of the People

Editors in alphabetical order by Christian Names
The Revd. Dr Andrew Sangster
The Revd. Christopher Ellis
Maurice Keys
The Revd. Canon Dr Peter Doll
The Revd. Canon Simon Wright

WHITE OWL
AN IMPRINT OF PEN & SWORD BOOKS LTD.
YORKSHIRE – PHILADELPHIA

First published in Great Britain in 2025 by
White Owl
An imprint of Pen & Sword Books Limited
Yorkshire – Philadelphia

ISBN 978 1 03619 515 1

A CIP catalogue record for this book is available from the British Library.

Typeset by Mac Style
Printed in the UK by CPI Group (UK) Ltd, Croydon, CR0 4YY.

MIX
Paper | Supporting responsible forestry
FSC® C013604

The Publisher's authorised representative in the EU for product safety is Authorised Rep Compliance Ltd., Ground Floor, 71 Lower Baggot Street, Dublin D02 P593, Ireland.
www.arccompliance.com

For a complete list of Pen & Sword titles please contact

PEN & SWORD BOOKS LIMITED
47 Church Street, Barnsley, South Yorkshire, S70 2AS, England
E-mail: enquiries@pen-and-sword.co.uk
Website: www.pen-and-sword.co.uk
or
PEN AND SWORD BOOKS
1950 Lawrence Road, Havertown, PA 19083, USA
E-mail: uspen-and-sword@casematepublishers.com
Website: www.penandswordbooks.com

Contents

Acknowledgements		vii
Preface		viii
Editorial Foreword		x
Introduction and Essential Articles		1
A Brief Historical Background to the Parish		4
The Parish: The Church of England on the Edge		7
Joined Up Parish Thinking		11
Loss of Faith		13
Loss of Religious Education		18
Finances in the Church of England		23
Episcopal Appointments		29
Freehold Independence or Controlled Employees?		33
Ordination Training		37
Chapter 1	Views of Clergy Still in Post	49
Chapter 2	Views of Retired Parish Clergy	89
Chapter 3	Lay Person's Response	117
Chapter 4	Letters From Those on the Edge of Parish Life	150
Chapter 5	Final Observations	165
Abbreviations and Glossary		175

Acknowledgements

The editors are spread between the Winchester, Norwich and York Dioceses, and contacted many in other dioceses, well over a hundred people across the English landscape. We are grateful to those who replied, and especially those who decided to contribute, and we fully understood why many who raised their heads above the parapet wanted to remain anonymous. We have received written letters and articles from a wide range of people, from a bishop and an army general, to retired clergy, many still serving, to full-time serving parish priests, lay people, and even those who never attend church but are conscious of the parish and the clergy serving therein. Their views had much in common, but not all, and the team of editors remain grateful for their contributions.

Preface

Emma Thompson, who is a member of the Steering Committee of the Save the Parish Movement (STP), wrote the following lines in *The Times* of 6 January 2025:

> We need someone who wants to spend time loving and caring for the downstairs church. By this, I mean the local places where people actually participate in and fund the Church. The upstairs church of bishops, bureaucracy and bluster has become inward-looking and detached from the parishes. It has grown on an indefensible scale. We need a parish-facing, pastoral archbishop, someone with the willingness and leadership ability to halve the upstairs church, scaling it back to a more appropriate and affordable level of overheads. There might then be some hope of reversing the decline that has been accelerated from within.

In the work of this project, we reflect the same issues but from a different perspective. We tend to use the military analogy of seeing the parish as the frontline troops and the upper echelons as military headquarters, but more to the point, we are mere unofficial assistants to the cause of the STP, and we are not taking a different angle but an innovative approach. After some explanatory articles on major issues, we are seeking the opinions of those who work or live within the parish system, not asking for a particular point of view but honest opinions from clergy and lay people including non-church goers. Some wish to remain anonymous, especially those in post, which is understandable given the climate of today. Our views are expressed by the title of the project, *From Barchester to Bedlam* (the publisher quite rightly changed the title to make more sense), but it is mainly written by those who have or are serving on 'the frontline'. This is not meant to be seen as an attack on the church as all the editors and many of the contributors have spent their lives serving the Church of England in one way or another. Some contributions have not been used for this reason as in some areas there is considerable anger, but this is an effort to provide a means for those who are or were active in the parish system to have their views heard. It is also essential to note that a particular 'line of thinking' was not requested, just honest views.

We have had a wide contribution, from an active bishop, a retired British Army general, and in Chapter Four (those on the fringe), some interesting insights by a local agnostic plumber, a non-church attending headteacher, and an atheistic medical doctor. Our effort is to give a voice to the people on 'the frontline' to draw attention to the problems relating to the crucial Christian work of parish life. The work of the STP is critical and it is hoped this effort will not just outline the problems, but demonstrate the true value of the parish system, and the need for the appropriate support.

Editorial Foreword

By the end of the year 2024 the Archbishop of Canterbury had resigned, and the Bishop of Newcastle appeared on television attacking the Archbishop of York, giving the appearance that the Church of England was in terms of leadership not only rudderless but in serious disarray and total confusion. There are many who feel that this is almost an irrelevance to the future of the Anglican Church compared to the apparent disintegration of the traditional parish system, which in reality, is the frontline for proclaiming the Gospel of Christ.

This has become clear with the Save the Parish movement and its website drawing attention to the growing chaos and doing its best to steady the ship. It has drawn attention to a number of poor decisions which have caused many of the current problems, and the list is lengthy. In 1976, the Endowment and Glebe Measure managed to transfer glebe land from parishes to the diocese, strengthening the diocese but weakening many parishes. Nor was the system helped with the abolition of freehold and creation of the idea of 'office holder', which for many clergy had an effect on their confidence and their sense of security, and today (February 2025) there has been talk of clergy becoming designated as 'employees', which is a strange word because most clergy feel themselves called by vocation, not looking for financial compensation for work loads.

Everyone within the Anglican Church is more than aware of the growth of diocesan authority and power, and there are wide ranging criticisms of the many well salaried appointments in the diocesan house, some of which are almost vague in their criteria. As one parish priest noted that when he saw the appointment for a spiritual guidance officer offering a major salary (noting it was called that and not a stipend) he asked if that were for the benefit of clergy, and he received the answer that it was the prime reason. He replied that for nearly fifty years he had been under the impression that his bishop was supposed to be his spiritual guidance person, as he was to his parishioners.

There is a growing awareness that the demand for the 'parish share' has become the major headache for parish clergy, and a new style of management has turned them from being parish priests caring for their community into minor management figures working for a head office. It has been reported by Save the Parish that as a general figure 21 per cent of expenditure goes towards diocesan support, and by reducing this by a mere 25 per cent would pay for nearly a thousand stipendiary clergy for frontline parish work.

It is known there is now a serious shortage of clergy, that parishes are being joined into large benefices, and there are parish shortfalls in financial payments to the diocese, which causes many to wonder about the long-term viability of the Anglican Church. Despite the efforts of Save the Parish many in the upper echelons of the hierarchy claim all is well within the parishes, which sounds more like a defensive strategy, as those on the frontline in the parish system, where good leadership is critical, know all too well that over the last twenty years the parish is not only changing, but it feels as if it could disintegrate. This is not mere pessimism but a genuine fear that without recognition of the facts about what is happening, it may be too late, but with a concerted effort it could be repaired and the work of God in the frontline parish continue.

This book is not the answer, nor is it a mere grumble, it simply outlines some of the issues, and it has sought the views of clergy and lay people working in parishes, thus the sub-title of *The Voice of the People*, because those on the frontline have more experience than the generals in the rear headquarters. It was not sent to people we knew to be unhappy, but a variety of contacts seeking other interested people. In other words, it was not sent to people with an 'axe to grind' but to those who knew about parish life.

Introduction and Essential Articles

In *The Times* on Friday, 11 October 2024 (p.12) the Bishop of Chelmsford, the Right Revd. Guli Francis-Dehqani stated that the Church had to accept that 'our numbers are declining, and influence is diminishing' and she criticised some senior colleagues for pursuing 'target driven strategies' to halt the decline. There is, she wrote, so much 'fear and anxiety' the Church was in danger of 'being sucked down a plughole of our own making'. She further argued by being 'fixated by the past we have lost and the future we dread', describing this as an 'exhausting cocktail'. She referred to the programme called *Vision and Strategy* for the 2020s to increase numbers, which she noted would put stress on overstretched clergy as they tried to increase numbers to be seen as successful. She further added that if dioceses want to access funding, they must prove they are supporting the strategy. The bishop explained she was not comfortable with the strategy because it reflected the secular business world. After Covid, Church statistics clearly indicate that numbers fell and have not recovered. She added that she agreed something has to be done, but not through 'setting targets'.

The Right Revd. Guli Francis-Dehqani is a bishop of our generation, but for many centuries the Church has been concerned about its seeming failures, and we must avoid looking back with rose-tinted glasses, even to the eighteenth and nineteenth centuries when there is a tendency to see the Church as flourishing and confident. In 1709, the well-known Dean Jonathan Swift wrote, 'Hardly one in a hundred among our people of quality or gentry appears to act by any principle of religion; great numbers of them do entirely discard it, and they are ready to own their disbelief of all revelation in ordinary discourse. Nor is the case much better among the vulgar.' In 1747, Bishop Butler (a well-known theologian, philosopher and writer) refused the Archbishopric of Canterbury, saying, 'It is too late to try and save a failing church'.

In the following century, Thomas Arnold (Rugby School headmaster and historian who supported the 'Broad Church Anglican' movement) wrote in 1832, 'The church as it now stands no human power can save'. In 1880, Bishop Ryle (an evangelical bishop and the first bishop of Liverpool) observed that 'the Church of England today is in a more critical and perilous position than at any period in the last two centuries. We are in rough waters, and whether or not we will weather the storm remains to be seen'. It is possible to see from these selected quotations from past centuries there was concern over the loss of faith, and a fear that the Church was becoming irrelevant.

However, the Church was still functioning in 1900 and although the First World War questioned the value of faith, and more recently Covid took its toll, it was and still is functioning. What we are facing today is more to do with the loss or weakening of the local parish system, which has become noticeable over the last twenty to thirty years. One of our contributors wrote in his email to us that he would express his views, but he felt it would be like knocking his head against a brick wall. Another asked 'why me?, I am only a parish priest in charge, not even a vicar or rector, ask the bishops and their henchmen the archdeacons.' When it was explained that the voice of those who had worked or are still working in the parish needed to be heard, someone joked and said it sounds like Lenin demanding to let the people speak. Those who have lived and are still living the parish life have the most experience about local community and presenting Christianity, even though they may be regarded as mere local foot soldiers of the cross. A military general may have maps on the wall, a reference book on strategy, tactics and an advisor on how to deal with political issues but very few would have a deep understanding of what it would be like to be a foot soldier on the frontline. Let us recall Sassoon's famous poem:

> 'Good-morning; good-morning!' the General said
> When we met him last week on our way to the line.

Now the soldiers he smiled at are most of'em dead,
And we're cursing his staff for incompetent swine.
'He's cheery old card,' grunted Harry to Jack
As they slogged up to Arras with rifle and pack.

But he did for them both by his plan of attack.

Many will say this is an unfair analogy, but this project is about the frontline workers expressing their views, which can hardly be done in the army, but the Church ought to find this more acceptable, given the working-class background of many of Christ's apostles. This is why when contributors were contacted, they were promised anonymity if they did not want to stick their heads above the parapet, and this has been respected. The original manuscript for this project bearing all names has been 'binned', so those who wanted to remain unknown can feel comfortable. No one particular line of view was asked for, just opinions, and many had much in common, but a few took a slightly different approach. These opinions have been studied by the editorial team, and the final chapter will summarise the majority feelings.

As part of the introduction certain areas of concern have been mulled over and raised in very short articles, mainly for reflective purposes. The first is naturally the background to the parish system, followed by what a parish is all about, and a brief one suggesting how enlarging benefices might function. The question is asked whether the decline in attendance amounts to a loss of faith, described by one historian as 'the unchurching of Europe', because it is not just a Church of England problem. This is followed by looking at the ramifications of the changes that have happened in the teaching of religion in schools. Several contributors raised the question of Church leadership, and another article was a survey of current bishops and their personal experience of parish life, which was something of an eye-opener for the editors. There have always been bishops with little or no parish experience, for example Archbishop Geoffrey Fisher, whose background was the world of public schools, but times have changed. Society is not structured as it was in his day. The present editors believe that recent and thorough experience of our society is best acquired by service at the coalface, which is the parish.

It was necessary to seek professional help over the question of Church finances, and the project team sought help from the website Save the Parish and were very grateful when they produced their contribution, written by a layman active within Church finances.

The main bulk of the work came from received contributions starting with parish clergy active at the moment, retired clergy, leading lay people, and some short ones from people who rarely if ever attend church, but who expressed opinions about living within a parish system. As noted, some wished to remain anonymous and the editorial team (spread across the country) looked for the common denominators summarised in the last chapter, Final Observations. Among the key points were the concerns raised about the loss of trained clergy, the question of financial demands, of moving towards the secular business world of management, blaming Covid, and neglecting the importance of local parish life.

The project team felt it necessary to remind readers of these findings, which do not arise from a quasi-revolutionary ecclesiastical political group making demands and challenging Church authority. We are all servants in our different ways of Jesus Christ who are deeply concerned about parish life and offer this project for reflection.

A Brief Historical Background to the Parish

The word parish can be traced back to ancient Greek and Latin, but it appeared in the English language of the thirteenth century arising from the Old French *paroisse*, with many possibilities of interpretation, but probably inferring 'that which is nearby', indicating the local area. Dating back to the late sixth to the early seventh centuries, it was regarded as part of the Church organisational system, and by the twelfth century stretched across the entire country. Villages would be a single parish, larger towns in time developed several, and if one lived out of the parish it was extra-parochial, although it was often the case that parishes had what may be described as 'detached parts'. The original burial ground, for example, may have been beyond the parish boundary. The parishes often had marker stones delineating their boundaries. This was important because the given Church land should not be taken back by the landowner or enlarged without consent, thus the later tradition of 'beating the bounds'. From the earliest times until the late nineteenth century many parishes were seen as reflecting known territorial areas, which was part of the country's organisation, but this association with landholding faded towards the end of the Middle Ages.

The parish system often started with a larger minster church with plenty of clergy ready to go out to perform their duties, but soon parishes with their own churches and priest became the norm. Even the concept of patronal oversight emerged at this time, as the local landowner who provided the land for the Church, the graveyard, and a home for the priest had the right of 'advowson', with the right of selecting a parish priest so long as the bishop agreed. The local parish priest later became known as the rector or vicar or even a perpetual curate. The clergy were soon given the title reverend but in many places the word father was and is still used. There was an early development of what we call a benefice, when one or two parishes were placed together as a unit, often with curates in the additional areas. Today the patron is not necessarily the landowner or local lord, it could be a bishop, a college, and many other institutions including the crown. Today appointments are governed by the Patronage (Benefices) Rules 1987. The bishop's oversight is important because the past has taught the dangers of some patrons wanting men to support their views, such as the demand for an evangelical priest, or an Anglo-Catholic version, while others may have had political demands such as a sound Tory or a good socialist.

It goes without saying that the system that had developed in the old Catholic Church, has survived intact through the Reformation. It soon developed its own organisational system, with what was often called a vestry committee, usually consisting of the local grandees. This led to the development under the Registration Act of 1 July 1836 when civil parish councils started to appear alongside Church parochial councils of today. To try and placate the various issues which inevitably arose with the myriad types of parishes, the office of the ecclesiastical commissioners was soon established. One of the features of the parish had been the appointment of a parish clerk who assisted the priest and church wardens in financial matters, and he assisted in the local church's poor law requirements. They were considered a major component so only a bishop or archdeacon could remove them from office. By the year 1835 there were 15,600 such parishes. It was the parish vestry committee that used to keep bridges and roads as usable, and helped the sick, the aged, and in the Elizabethan era this was even regularised. From the sixteenth to the eighteenth century the parish was a stabilising influence, especially in resolving disputes which some have pinpointed as the early signs of democracy. There was a fine line between the work of the vestry meeting and secular work which is why the development of the civic parish councils was so important. The parish church is often the largest or tallest building in the area, and more often than not it is the most historic building which helped indicate the importance the parish played within its given community. The parish with its priest and vestry committee was fundamental to the life of every community, especially in rural areas.

By the late twentieth century to this day there has been a decline in both parish priests and the worshipping communities, and many parish churches do not have a regular Sunday worship, and many are led by lay people. People have varying views on this development of lay leadership. When lay people are trained to assist in worship it is undoubtedly a good thing, but as has been experienced in America there is a danger that a charismatic lay person can produce his or her own cult, as they are not under the episcopal control as a priest should be, and they cannot or should not conduct sacramental services.

During the last fifty years the traditional Church of England parish system is acknowledged to be in decline for a variety of possible reasons. The first may well be the loss of faith, the fall in ordination candidates, and the decline of theological colleges. The latter two are critical as committed and well-trained clergy may just possibly help stop the decline in worshiping numbers. The lack of committed clergy has meant the widening of benefices for financial reasons, some sound theological colleges were closed for the same money-type problems. The parish system served this country for over a thousand years, and it is worth preserving primarily because it brings the love of God into the community and serves that area as a major focus of local life.

This study does not set out to put much energy into the data and facts which in this modern age are easily obtainable, but to seek the views of parish people, the clergy, the lay people who assist, the worshippers, and those who never attend a service. It is the people's voice which should be heard.

The Parish: The Church of England on the Edge

The parish was never designed by anyone, it just grew naturally. From the earliest times Christian missionaries and leaders have lived and worked among the communities they sought to serve. This is entirely as it should be as the place where a person lays his or her head at night is the place where they are most themselves. It is where they live and so also the place where their faith which means the most to them can flourish.

This rather obvious observation describes what lies beneath the idea of the Anglican parish. It is this basic idea that has always helped to keep the Church in touch. The history of the Church in these islands has seen many ups and downs. There has been much abuse of privilege and misuse of power. There have been plenty of divisions and bitter arguments, but there has always been the expectation that the Church is present among us and has things to say about the way we live, both as individuals and communities.

Now things have changed. The English parish no longer has the same place in people's lives. If someone had proposed the idea of a campaign to Save the Parish forty or fifty years ago, people would have thought they were mad. The parish was a given fact of everyday life. Most people were baptised and married in the parish church and expected to have their funerals there. Church registers did not just record religious or liturgical acts but crucial life events, which is why they are so valuable to family researchers. Far more people attended Sunday worship, and while the majority of the population have never been regular worshippers, except when it was compulsory, Church worship was seen as a normal part of community life. There were plenty of occasional worshippers, who assumed the Church would always be there. The Church of England has always been healthily fuzzy around the edges. It has never kept strict membership records.

It was also normal for the Church to be involved in major community events. Even as recently as 1981, the Archbishop of York was asked to bless the Humber Bridge when it was opened. Throughout the country, the local vicar would have been expected to be present at all major community events. In the long extinct magazine *Picture Post,* an edition published in 1948 featured the article *The Life of a Country Parson*. In it there was a photograph of the Revd. J.G. Wright keeping the score at a skittle match in the local village. Such things are less likely or normal today. One of the editors had a parish with the naval dockyards, and he was always asked to say the prayers when a new vessel was launched.

It is only fair to say that some clergy found such things irksome and a distraction from their religious duties, but it is an assumption of this study that the church's involvement with the community was both healthy and fruitful. There was a continuing relationship between the community and the Church, which was largely maintained by the activities and presence of the parish priest.

It is not like that anymore. There are a number of reasons why this change has occurred. Many of them are nothing to do with the Church and are beyond its control. There is the growth of secularism, the appearance of other religions, a growing scepticism about all institutions, including Parliament and the monarchy amongst other things. There are also ways in which the Church has been its own worst enemy or has not responded well to changes in society.

There has been an overall reduction in the numbers coming forward for ordination. At the same time there has been a growing worry about how to pay and house them. In considering this, the role of the Church commissioners needs to be questioned. How did the budgetary crisis come about so suddenly and why was it not foreseen? This is a specialist area of study, but it seems odd that the commissioners could fund so much more a few years ago and cannot do so now. Is it just the result of economic changes in the world, or have certain policy decisions made the difference? In this general introduction there will be another sub-section surveying the financial issues.

Another major factor has been the change in the way parish ministry is approached. There has been the extremely healthy and welcome development in lay ministry. It is the recognition that the Church is the whole community of faith, and it is not just a clerical enterprise. In this respect it has moved nearer the principles set out by Paul in I Corinthians Verse 12 concerning the gifts of the spirit. One significant sign of this has been the change of designation for the priest leading the Eucharist, who is now called the 'President' rather than the 'celebrant'. It acknowledges that the whole Church celebrates this act. All this is extremely healthy and good, but it has raised new issues.

One question is the role of the ordained ministry. With many lay people taking on roles previously seen as mainly the role of the clergy, we need to ask how the clergy and laity work together. Historically lay people have always been involved in pastoral care in informal ways, but the parish priest was primarily seen as the pastor. Also lay people have always led worship, with church wardens being able to read morning or evening prayer if the priest is unavailable. There is also the enormous contribution made by lay readers over the years. Now, because of the shortage of priests, there is much non-eucharistic worship which is lay led often by people who come forward locally. Some go through training in their diocese and receive authorisation, while others act without any selection, training, or authorisation. While many of them may do excellent work, but this may not always be true and there does need to be some way of ordering matters in a better way.

Pastoral care is another area of major concern. The ordinal makes it noticeably clear that this is a key role of the priest, which is now proving problematic. Many clergy do not undertake regular parish visiting, either because they feel they do not have time or because they do not think it is an effective use of their energy. In days gone by curates were encouraged to spend most of their time visiting and many continued this when they became incumbents. That does not always happen today, and it is a huge loss to the Church, so it is worth trying to describe the benefits of parish visiting. The major beneficiary was the visitor. He or she would learn about the community, its families, and individuals. The visitor would get to know its history and its attitudes and current issues. A parish priest who visited regularly could well acquire a better knowledge of the parish than anyone else in the area.

A parish priest has a representative role. He or she is a visible, physical sign that the Church is present in that community and that there is a worshipping, praying community there. This means that God is there in their midst. The visitor achieves an introduction and an implied invitation. Often, visiting does not have a directly 'religious' purpose. A priest might offer to pray at a house or might be asked to say a prayer, but more often they would simply visit the people, get to know them, and hopefully show them that they are respected and valued. Wise priests might be skilled in initiating conversations, but thereafter they would allow the parishioner to set the agenda. Even though this kind of visiting was, and still sometimes is, undertaken for the reasons given, it was in reality highly evangelistic. It is not an alternative to pastoral actions undertaken by lay people but should be seen in conjunction. Visiting would often start with matters like the electoral roll, the baptism and funeral registers, but would usually expand so that new contacts were made.

With both worship and pastoral care someone needs to lead, and we need to find a way for parish priests to do this even though their numbers are reduced. Leadership in this setting is not about dominance or rank but cooperation and enablement. We also need to keep hold of the insights and skills learnt in the past and find ways of applying them in present conditions. One obvious thing which has been said many times is the need to free clergy from administrative tasks. The danger at present is that they find themselves acting as benefice managers rather than pastors. For example, does every tiny village need a parochial church council (PCC), church wardens, and treasurer? Do we need a root and branch review of the whole legal structure of the system?

Recent years have seen the growth in the numbers of self-supporting clergy. This has been a huge help in many areas where ordained ministers are few on the ground, but it has serious limitations. First, it is difficult to use them strategically because they are likely to minister near where they live. Secondly, they are limited in their opportunities to gain experience. Stipendiary clergy often used to serve two curacies in different parishes and would gain a lot of experience in the process. This provided time for reflection and development in their own understanding of their ministry. It is often argued that self-supporting ministers bring valuable experience from their secular lives, but there is no guarantee of this. Their secular work and experience may not be truly relevant, and even if it is, it needs to be interpreted and integrated into their ministry. Finally, with the best will in the world they will always be limited by their other responsibilities.

In all these ways the Church finds itself on the edge. In many areas it is providing service cover rather than parish ministry. Perhaps the Church of England needs to rediscover the truth that it is here to serve; that surely is its vocation.

Joined Up Parish Thinking

For many years dioceses have been joining parishes together, usually to form a united benefice. This has been in response to the shortage of ordained clergy to staff and support them, especially with the lack of resources. Thus, we now have many large units of many parishes, often looked after by one priest who may well be a house of duty appointment and part-time. There has been the suggestion that the Church should develop a minster style of working, having ministers based at a central point or hub and serving the 'outlying' areas from there. This may have been tried in some places, but none are known to have been established in this writer's area.

The policy of just joining parishes together has some implications. First it means people go to Church less often. This is because in large groups of parishes, it is not possible to have services in every church each Sunday. Some will manage two services in the morning and one later in the day. Some will say that the service is in such and such a church this week and encourage all parishioners to come, regardless of where they live, which for many, especially for the older participants, may cause problems.

Ideally people would travel to where the main service is, and it would provide a much better experience for all. In practice only a minority manage to do this. Most just go when the service is in what they may call 'their own' church. The result is that many people have lost the habit of weekly Sunday church attendance. It undoubtedly also effects the giving. There will be honourable exceptions to this pattern, but it is all too clearly observable in many places.

As noted above, there may be a number of reasons why people find it so difficult to go to a different church, particularly in the country. They may not have transport, and there may be ancient rivalries between villages. In some places there may be class differences with some villages, being, in their own eyes at least, a 'bit posher' than the one down the road. Some words from John Betjeman's poem *Blame the Vicar* come to mind:

> The living's been amalgamated
> With the one next door they've always hated.

A more positive reason may be that people are concerned for the life of their village. It may have lost its pub, its shop, and the church is the one thing that provides its identity and character. Many value the presence of the church even if they do not feel they need to attend.

Alongside these problems, parish clergy struggle with the need to maintain the structures. Finding people to serve as church wardens, treasurers, and in other capacities, which is also very difficult, especially in very small parishes. Many are known to manage with just one church warden, who may well occupy other offices as well.

Perhaps the time has come for this invaluable tradition for the Church to seek a radical look at the parish system to find a new way of doing the administration that does not use so many resources. Perhaps in some places it might be sensible to have one PCC for the whole benefice, one set of officers for the whole group, possibly with the local church wardens making up the PCC along with a few others. It would have to be approached with great care to avoid some parishes feeling they were not being downgraded, but the object would be to focus as many resources as possible on providing local Christian ministry. Finance would be crucial and ideally a united parish, as opposed to a united benefice, would combine finances. This would be hard to achieve but could have dramatic advantages.

Sometimes people make the mistake of thinking that if the services are covered, then the parish is being ministered to. This is not really true. It is the work that goes on in the week that matters, and this is what maintains and builds up congregations. With more time freed from administration those clergy we are fortunate to have would be able to spend more time with parishioners in their homes and in local activities. Lay people would be freer to serve Jesus Christ and witness to the love of God in their communities. With the grace of God, it might maintain the invaluable Church of England tradition of providing ministry that is primarily local and pastoral.

Loss of Faith

Historians often use the phrase 'the unchurching of Europe' frequently pointing out that the process started after the devastating disaster of the the Great War, with the evident implication that belief in God had not helped avert the disaster. This may be something of an oversimplification of the issue, especially when some were convinced that they saw the angel of God over the Mons battlefield in 1914, and the Germans wore *Gott mit uns* (God is with us) on their belts and many banners. The loss of faith across Europe has continued unabated and today many of the traditional churches and non-conformist chapels are closed and used for many purposes other than worship. In this writer's city some medieval churches are used as bookshops, cafés, a puppet theatre, one old church advertising a 'non-religious wedding' venue, a martial arts centre, and in other places they have become night clubs with many more rural churches slowly crumbling away to ivy clad ruins.

From the last century to this day there has been a significant decline not just in church attendance but a notable loss of faith in a Godhead. In 2001, the general census included a question about faith for the first time, and 72 per cent still identified themselves as Christian and 15 per cent claimed no-religion. It is impossible to verify by ticking 'Christian' whether it was meant as coming from that background or social politeness. In the days when a hospitalised patient would be asked to which religion they belonged the automatic answer was often C of E. One thing is certain on reflecting on this census, that the above 72 per cent never attended places of worship, raising the question as to why the Church is losing members. It must be understood that many people still have a form of faith but have no desire to worship. It is also true that many who have drifted away from the Church have done so on the basis of an inaccurate perception of the Church. With less Christian influence and also less personal contact with a church, people form an idea that it is based on other things. For example, in many TV dramas clergy are often depicted in odd ways, such as creeping round their churches lighting candles, and rarely are they shown out and about doing pastoral work. In the series *Grantchester* for example the parish priest hero spends most of his time solving crimes with the local police inspector. When we see him in church, he is usually standing in the middle aisle addressing the congregation about his personal problems.

It is widely accepted that the two world wars with their dominant secular ideologies (communism and fascism) and even some aspects of existentialism did not help. The various churches were aware of the drop in numbers, and it appears today that less than 5 per cent ever attend worship. Efforts were made by the ecumenical movement, there were evangelical outreaches, the charismatic arrival all played a role, and preachers such as Billy Graham 'had their day', but the downward fall of church attendance remains a grave issue for believers. Notable in most churches are the lack of younger people, often brought up in non-attending church families, and many having no form of religious teaching in their schools (see article on school religious education). British society is becoming multi-cultural, but despite the bigoted fears of many, the major population remains Christian by background, but this does not mean they attend church or have any faith.

Trying to find statistics which are dependable is not only difficult, but reading what they offer can be interpreted in diverse ways. However, it is generally known that both Protestantism in its various shades, and Roman Catholicism have been in long-term decline, and it is similar in many American churches, not least in the once all-powerful Southern Baptist Convention.

In the *Time* magazine of 8 April 1966, the cover asked, 'Is God Dead?'

This question raises the issue as to whether there is a loss of faith in God's existence by countless individuals for personal reasons, or has the Church failed. The writer Tom Holland in his book *Dominion, The Making of the Western Mind* (Publisher Abacus, 2020) suggests the Christian faith has transformed into a form of secular life in terms of human equality, charitable work, social care has fulfilled its key role and requires no form of mourning. A separate way of looking at the problem is to repeat the question is the loss of faith in God the fault of the Church or a change in the so-called perspective of modern life.

Putting aside the role of the Church it is necessary to explore some of the reasons why people jettison their faith in God. This can often be speculation, but talking with atheists, agnostics, and especially those who have walked away offers some interesting insights. It is known that when faced with major disasters such as war, nearly always brought about by human initiative through our own free will, it is often the case that belief in a Godhead falls when prayers go seemingly unanswered. These 'disasters' can range from major wars to pandemics such as Covid, racial hatred, political oppression, accidents, with some recently mentioning climate change in a world they took as God's creation, blaming God and not humankind's behaviour. The warning signs of climate have been many and prolonged, demanding international cooperation, but humankind is constantly failing and many blame it on God instead of human leaders and their followers. It stems from the human inability to understand, from the religious point of view that God's gift to mankind was free will, and we make the choices.

As a race we always, and perhaps understandably, find personal suffering difficult, and for many the lesson of carrying the cross has become meaningless. One man told the writer he had stopped worshiping God when he fell into debt through no fault of his own but because of the greed of others, and God did nothing about his dilemma despite constant prayers. When tragically another acquaintance's only child committed suicide for no apparent reason to him or his wife, this horror finished his hitherto life-long attendance at worship. It is impossible not to feel sympathetic to a person suffering from personal loss and deep trauma, and it feels like an imposition to suggest free will and God has given us that freedom. Such a victim needs human love and sympathy with the hope that this is interpreted as God reaching out, but for many this carries little weight. As a young boy the writer recalls promising God that if he passed his GCEs he would attend evensong for every Sunday for the next five years. It was a childish bargain like the man who every time he placed a bet on the horses held a small crucifix in his hand. This is a human failing that can change the course of our lives. Some find comfort in the idea that God is with them in their suffering. While this is true of orthodox Christian teaching, it does not always provide the comfort people seek.

Those who were once regular attenders often feel challenged by the seeming complexities in the Bible, and many lifelong priests have walked through this valley of doubt. It is a failure to understand that although the Bible is understood to be the word of God it was written by his servants, and scholars of ancient texts know that that even some of the most sacred texts have been changed for a variety of human reasons.

We live in a world where science is regarded as explaining everything, even though there is no explanation as to why there is something and not a vacuum, that a complex form of life exists and all we can do is wonder where else in the solar system this may have happened. Despite the intricacy of being alive and aware of the complexity of the human body and life, many people believe that science is the only answer. It is an ancient problem and the old arguments for God's existence such as the ontological to the teleological and many others are ignored for the scientific microscope. When occasionally the local atheist raises this point of dependency upon science it seems to make sense to many people and sadly the response is too often muted.

Many people are only happy if they can have empirical evidence that we are not a mistake of biochemistry but a carefully created form of life. This is an issue that has always dogged human thinking and will never go away. These intellectual doubts are challenging and those who remain believers often fail to reach the challenge in debate as more people turn their backs on belief. Sadly, another reason for loss of faith in the Christian way of life has been 2,000 years of hypocrisy, ineptness, and the moral failures of religious institutions and leaders. The history of the Church makes for indigestible reading, neglecting the fact that although it is God's Church it is run by us, mere mortals, free will again. This has recently raised it head with issues over safeguarding and the immoral deviancy of a few clergy, which has led to the resignation of the Archbishop of Canterbury and quarrels between senior bishops.

The Church of England

This question of the loss of faith can apply to all religions, and as with the Christian Church to the various splinter groups or denominations, but this project is looking towards the Church of England. The English established Church is a wide umbrella as it is well known by its different approaches to worship, ranging from the evangelical wing to Anglo-Catholics with a wide variety of options in between. In many ways it has almost become part of the Church fabric and accepted by most adherents, but for some as unfortunate, but 'one of those things' because we all worship differently, some Anglo-Catholic other Evangelicals, and this should be respected. However, over recent years there have been various conflicts which have deterred many from passing through church doors. These debates have led to fragmentation and often too much heat. There have been many internal conflicts which have not been good for those on the edge of belief. There was the debate over women priests, gay clergy, same-sex marriage, female bishops, all of which gave many a poor impression of the Church, mainly because of the vitriolic venom deployed. During the Covid pandemic when churches were closed many people withdrew and some decided home felt better and safer than the pew.

When efforts were made to halt the decline such as in 1975 with the *Call to the Nation* launched by the Archbishop of Canterbury and a decade of Evangelism it has proved ineffective. It all gives the impression that the Church of England does not seem relevant to the general public, especially the younger generation. Some have suggested that the last archbishop's somewhat gloomy approach has not helped, and the occasional exposure of sexual misconduct by a few clergy has changed many attitudes. It was something of a theological irony that as this brief article was first being prepared the collect for the day started with 'Keep, we beseech Thee, O Lord, Thy Church with Thy perpetual mercy: and, because the frailty of man without Thee cannot but fail…' (Trinity XV).

It is clear that Christianity in England is far from over, and the main hope is with the work of the priest and Christian lay people deep in every community, namely the work of the parish. Once the parish priest took 90 per cent of funerals and weddings, and baptism took place every weekend. Now humanists take more funerals mainly because undertakers find them easier to contact and they do not charge as much. This is not the intention at this stage to open this particular debate, but when looking back over the years it becomes clear if the loss of faith is to be addressed it is best done within the parish community, which is the keynote to addressing the problem of the loss of faith.

Loss of Religious Education

Historical Backdrop

In schools today and of the recent past, RE has had a variety of titles, ranging from religious instruction (RI), religious knowledge (RK) to divinity and many others. The nomenclature of this subject is wider than all the other academic subjects put together. For the sake of ease, RE in this brief survey will be used to cover all groupings. In terms of the long overview and before the state took an interest in schooling, nearly all teaching stemmed from the Christian Church. When the 1870 Education Act was passed the state took an interest in education, because, according to some commentators it was a response to ecclesiastical conflicts of the day. Prior to 1870, three-quarters of grant-aided schools were Anglican and carried immense influence. The non-conformists became more politically powerful and in 1814 started the British and Foreign School Society. The Emancipation Act of 1829 allowed the Roman Catholics to start their Poor School Committee, and until recent times the various Christian churches were influential, most especially in the teaching of RE. The teaching at this stage was largely confessional, meaning the teaching of each denominational school was a form of instruction in what to believe about God. However, there was considerable tension between the denominations and in 1902, an act was passed extending aid to Church schools, but with the complaint that the established Church of England had dominated the scene and gained the most.

By the 1930s, following the disaster of the Great War interdenominational relations indicated an easing of the tensions, and in 1936 another Education Act helped the churches provide senior schools. Before this, in 1929, Pope Pius XI produced an Encyclical Letter called *Divini Illius Magistri* which stated that education was about forming the perfect Christian, and he also rejected religious mixed schools, a question still raising problems.

This was followed by the (Sir William) Spens Report (1938) dividing senior schools between grammar, technical, and modern. It also regarded RE as having moral purposes, which made it difficult as an examinational subject, and it raised the issue of the lack of experienced teaching staff. There followed the Norwood Report (1943), which drew a distinction between scripture knowledge and religious information, and which was objective and therefore examinational.

In the 1944 Education Act the people behind this were hoping not just for a fairer and wider educational system, but with a Christian and moral hope for an improved post-war era. In 1959, there was the Crowther Report which stated that teenagers with whom we are concerned need, perhaps more than anything else, 'to find a faith by which to live by'. By the 1988 act the politicians were seeking a 'good citizen programme'. The subject of RE received more attention than any other subject, and it has long been a subject of debate in political and educational circles. In 1992/93 there was a white paper called *Choice and Diversity* that revealed many issues over the teaching of the subject, which were never satisfactorily resolved and with no signs of a consensus of opinion. In the second half of the last century although the teaching of RE was a legal necessity, there was a growing debate over precisely what the subject was meant to achieve, whether it was simply meant to be confessional, as Pope Pius XI demanded. Many wanted unmixed religious schools that taught the Christian faith through their denominational eyes; others, on the other hand, demanded it to be taught as an objective academic examinational subject, which demanded a knowledge of religion and religious beliefs.

As a subject it was virtually side-lined by being removed from the national curriculum and left to the local authority, so each had a standing advisory council of the subject, known as SACREs. Governments statistics clearly show that between 2018 and 2021, the number of pupils taking RE at GCSE and A-Level had dropped considerably. In 2018, Charles Clarke (former Secretary of Education) produced a pamphlet claiming RE in schools was outdated and should be replaced by religion, belief and values. In 2016, there was the Commission on Religious Education as there was a growing demand to overhaul Religious Education, looking for pupils to understand the relationship between people's world views and their thinking and actions in political, public, social and cultural life. The National Association for Teachers of Religious Education (NATRE) in 2017 reported that more than a quarter of England's secondary schools did not offer RE which would be contravening the law. If the 2016 commission is followed, more schools would drop the subject because it would need more skilful academics to teach such a change.

The denominational tensions had not been resolved by the 1870 act and as the next century followed politicians became involved, with continuing uncertainty about the subject of RE and it is rapidly becoming an academic non-starter, its variations demanded by different SACREs making it even more confusing as a respectable subject worthy of pursuit.

Ramifications Today

This writer can easily recall in 1950–56 attending a Church of England primary school with an assembly every day and a subject called religious instruction. Twice a week the parish priest, known as Father Budgen, would take the assembly, and he always came across well with the boys and girls because he was friendly and at times amusing, reminding us that if we joined the church choir, we could be given two shillings each month, and half a crown if there were five Sundays in the month. He told us if we could not sing then we would be taught how to serve at the altar, no one was excluded. In the senior school the subject was called religious knowledge, and it was different from the primary school because it appeared much more academic, teaching about the Gospels, what the Epistles were all about, and later the exciting stories from the Old Testament, resulting in one large boy being called Goliath, a nickname he carried to his death. The subject was almost exciting, and this writer thought it easy and took it at A-Level and went onto sit the old-fashioned BD degree only to find it meant studying *koine* Greek and classical Hebrew. Later, the same school started to teach comparative religions which made sense in a growing multi-cultural society, but finding staff was eventually impossible and the whole subject was dropped.

This writer spent seven years as a school chaplain in one of New Zealand's top private schools (public schools in English terminology) teaching divinity, Latin, and English literature. The New Zealand state schools, unlike the private schools had by an 1877 law abandoned the teaching of RE, and at a conference there were complaints that teaching the works of John Milton was proving difficult because of Milton's constant biblical allusions, which youngsters (and many teachers) with no biblical knowledge found difficult to manage. Later, at a synod in the Wellington diocese there was debate about the Anglican Church's support of private schools as for some it appeared unfair. One speaker asked the house of clergy to raise their hands if they had attended a private school and an enormous majority had, resolving the debate in favour of continuing support.

Whether a person is committed to the Christian faith or is atheistic is a personal choice, but ignorance of religious belief is as bad as not knowing one's history, and it is evidently detrimental to a sound education. In England, the subject is now low on the interest basis and mainly controlled by politically based local authorities. Christianity, for all its faults and at times unpleasant history, is part of our background, and in a growing multi-cultural society there should also be an element of some knowledge in comparative religions, but finding the teaching expertise is now a challenging task.

Church schools still exist, but they are only a part of a national system which has demoted RE to a lowly position on the academic scale. There are also further ramifications as most religions, some more than others, have a history of not just how a country formed, but which established a moral basis as to how people should behave. Being a Church going Christian, as experience has shown, does not necessarily produce good people with high moral standards, but it sets watermarks for the conscience of growing youngsters. In the recent (Southport) street riots of the summer of 2024 when mosques and hotels holding immigrants were viciously attacked, prompted by misleading news and extreme toxic right-wing fanaticism, most people were horrified. In this writer's city all was quiet, but on speaking to a young man the writer was told that the protests against immigrants should have been more widespread. When he was asked about the good samaritan he had never heard of the parable, and when asked about 'loving my neighbour as myself' the prompt reply was 'they are not the neighbours I want'. It was like hitting a brick wall. The writer recalled the early post-war years of 1950 when Father Budgen, mentioned above, was the parish priest keeping on about the good samaritan and told the children to 'get back to playing cowboys and Indians', and to stop playing 'German and Tommy' and treat the boys in the Roman Catholic school down the road as neighbours as well.

The teaching of RE gave a background to the faith, some knowledge of Christianity, but also provided some moral standards to challenge our behaviour. It helped when the parish priest caught our attention because of his strange black shirt and sense of friendly authority. We all have to accept that times are changing, and later in life when this writer was a headmaster suffering an Ofsted visit, he asked the lead woman what she thought about the RE department, only to hear the reply that it was low on their agenda, they were only curious, and it was 'political dynamite'. The loss of the old fashioned RE has been part of the diminishing loss of faith, but it has scarred the intellectual strength of many young people.

Finances in the Church of England

In the Beginning – A Financial Roller Coaster

In the beginning the life of a parish priest was much simpler: they were able to undertake 'the cure of souls' in its fullest sense, now this often comes secondary to coping with an avalanche of dictates and papers from on high, training courses and the like and trying to raise the parish share, not forgetting keeping the church in good order. Their income might have been derived from a variety of sources including donations, endowments, glebe land or family money. This changed when the Endowments and Glebe Measure Act 1976 came into force. The diocese took over the assets of the parish church and in return every incumbent in England received a regular stipend. It was still expected that parishes would contribute towards the stipend of their incumbent, expenses and housing in part or full via the giving they received. Giving by parishioners has always been voluntary but over the years it has transformed itself into the biggest source of church income and into benefice quotas, otherwise called parish share, which include a contribution to diocesan running costs. The diocese now apportions the total parish share on an annual basis to benefices. Failure to pay in part or full brings the archdeacon knocking on a priest's front door!

The 1976 act was a positive move and resolved several anomalies in the then system. The same, with hindsight, is not true of the subsequent Financial Settlement Act of 1997. Under this act it was agreed that the Church commissioners would continue to pay the pensions of stipendiary clergy already in their system. Henceforth from the 1 January 1998 the dioceses, through their Diocesan Boards of Finance (DBF), would become responsible for all new pensions. This worked well, at least for the Church commissioners, who given the respite they had asked for and acknowledging, they then embarked on a better investment programme, have grown their assets from £3.5bn to a current £10.4bn. Unfortunately, the same cannot be said for the DBFs who have increasingly struggled with the payment of stipends, housing and pension payments. It is estimated that the pension cost to the DBFs since the system changed is currently £2.6bn.

Now let us examine the Church finances and money streams in a little more detail. It may be helpful to look at the diagram below, taken from the Save the Parish website. I am deliberately starting at the top of the pyramid, given the current managerial nature of the Church, with the Church commissioners and the Archbishops' Council.

Church Commissioners/Archbishops' Council

Money is power and there is no doubt that the Church has money – £10.4bn and that currently power rests with these two bodies. I say this because first as the commissioners not only fund pre-1998 pensions, bishops and cathedral clergy stipends but make money available to the central church via the triennium funding scheme. In the period 2023/25 they pledged £1.2bn with a commitment, subject to their investment income, of maintaining this level over the next two triennia to give a total of £3.6bn. Whether this money is spent wisely and to best effect is subject to debate. Monies made available under the Lower Income Community Grant scheme have largely been used for their intended purpose, i.e. to support and develop mission in communities with the most deprived populations. However, much has been 'wasted' on failed schemes. Sir Robert Chote in one of the few reports that followed the money and was made public, reported in 2022 that the then Strategic Investment Board's grant of £176.7m aimed at winning new disciples, had so far spent £74.5m and as far as could be determined had 'won' 12,705 new disciples against a final target of 89,375. The rest of the money followed, and the best estimate is it achieved 27,500 new disciples

– though some of these were Church plants. Had this money been used to fund parish priests then it could have paid for up to 250 parish priests for 10 years including stipends, pension and housing. Another example was the way in which training for ministry courses was funded from 2017. Despite warnings from theological educational institutions that the system of giving money to dioceses and allowing them to manage their budget was flawed it still went ahead. The 2022 review found that the TEI's fears amongst others were well founded. The system was not working, and dioceses were accumulating money estimated to reach £4m by summer 2022. Fortunately, the General Synod agreed a funding revision in February 2023.

Church of England – Cash Flow Diagram

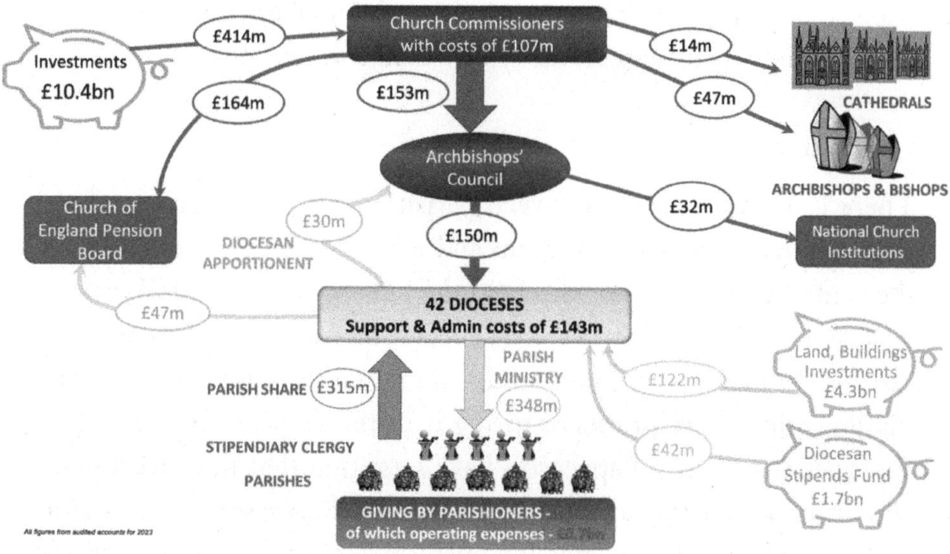

Diocese and Parishes

Although parishes have little or no assets, they are the major contributor to the Church raising £1,055bn in 2022 (based on 2022 being the latest published church parish statistics), in parish share, tax rebates, repairs to church buildings, legacies, investment income and trading. As shown above in 2023 parish share totalled £315m (£318m in 2022) with parish ministry costing £348m. As well as the parish ministry of £348m the dioceses paid £47m for pensions, £30m to the Archbishops' Council and £143m administration costs etc. totalling £568m, giving a shortfall of £253m. However, they received £164m from glebe land and investments, as well as £150m from the Archbishops' Council leaving a surplus of £61m. Despite this with the fall in Church attendees, giving, failing to maximise investments and increased support costs, most dioceses, i.e. thirty are in deficit when looking at their general income and expenditure.

Finally, be aware that the Archbishops' Council determines how the money it receives is passed by way of grants. Previously, until 2015 money was allocated under the Darlow formula, but it was then changed to a grant application system. General Synod has little or no say in how grant monies are allocated: if your diocese can write a good story the chances are you will be on a winner. Grant awards tend to focus on diocesan applications that project increases in Church members. Current Church membership would suggest the system is not working!

Conclusions

There is a stark contrast between parishes struggling to meet all the financial demands made on them and a 'head office', i.e. dioceses and the central church bodies who hold the bulk of the assets. We seem to be able to find money for a slavery reparation fund – £100m, Net Zero 2030 – £190m and racial justice triennium funding £20m; anything but funding stipendiary priests or giving it to the parishes. In the current 'managerial system' we appear to have forgotten that the parish priest and the parish are the lifeblood of the Church. So, we see administrators such as diversity officers, mission enablers, archdeacons' assistants and even bishops continually increasing and at what cost, whilst stipendiary clergy numbers continue to decrease – in 2020 the total was 7,670 and in 2023 estimated at circa 7,000.

Fortunately, there seems to be a slow but increasing awareness of the problem. The recently appointed new chair of the Archbishops' Finance Committee, Carl Hughes tabled a paper in July last regarding the state of the diocesan finances with more to follow. It remains to be seen what changes will be made and how a new archbishop of Canterbury will respond to the challenges. Starting at the bottom and working upwards might be the way forward?

Editorial Comment: No one in the project team, most of whom have struggled with parish finances over the recent years, had any real knowledge of the national picture of the Church of England's finances, except to know that there was a deepening struggle to pay the parish quota, causing deep concern and taking many hours of work and persuasion. We turned to the Save the Parish movement for help. As a team we were very grateful for their positive response and one of their members who wrote this article.

To conclude this section on money it has been pointed out that aspects of Church life are often reflected in the press, and attached is a brief letter sent by a curious member of the public.

Attracting Public Attention

Since I am an old and a retired widow the most pleasure that I have is watching TV and reading the papers and gossiping at the church hall's coffee morning. We, the coffee circle, have noted the press and media have also been alerted to the problems facing the Church of England, because of the resignation of the Archbishop of Canterbury, the television recorded the bitter attack of the Bishop of Newcastle on the Archbishop of York, but the sudden resignation of the Bishop of Liverpool over alleged sexual misconduct by another bishop caused us an unpleasant surprise. Headlines and investigative journalists feed on this mayhem, and it does the Church little good in the public eye. As the vitriolic debates over gay clergy, women priests, and the failures in Covid drew criticism onto the Church. We asked ourselves if this meant the Church was weak from the roots, or is it overbearing leadership, being a mere congregational member gives me no real knowledge, but I gather there are problems about Church leadership. However, it is also becoming widely known that the Church of England not only has serious financial problems, but that the question of money by those in charge is not being dealt with in the best possible way regarding the survival of parish churches.

In the *Church Times* on 4 February 2025, a copy left by our rector, written by Revd. Marcus Walker a member of the General Synod for London diocese wrote a letter seeking support for the need to keep all parishes, even the impoverished ones, and sustained as the top priority. The entire article contained the following extracts [this letter arrived in its original form cut from the *Church Times,* with some extracts underlined in red]:

> The poor will always be with us, but will we always be with the poor? For centuries, the Church of England has known that poorer parishes cannot be expected to fund from their own resources. Queen Anne knew this and set up an endowment: the famous Queen Anne's Bounty 'for the augmentation of the Maintenance of the Poor Clergy'
>
> Parliament got in on the act with the Ecclesiastical Commissioners, and the two endowments are now joined and looked after by the Church Commissioners. Their portfolio stands at more than £10 billion, and the income from that money is supposed to be ring-fenced and spent, to quote the governing statute, 'with particular regard to ... the making of additional provision for the cure of souls in parishes where such assistance is most required'.
>
> But, as churches close and merge, and parishes are stripped of clergy, one pattern has started to become clear: the brunt of this is being borne by the poor. The Church Buildings Council has shown that 40 per cent of church closures take place in the ten per cent most deprived parishes, and that churches in the ten per cent most deprived are five times as likely to close as churches in the least deprived quintile. [Quintile is a statistical value of data that represents 20 per cent of a population.]
>
> Rebalancing our funding to avoid the demise of poor parishes will not mean that everything else has to come to a stop: it just means that the Church absolutely has to consider whether those poorest

> parishes, which will never be able to fund themselves, are properly provided for. Then it can spend the rest of the money elsewhere.
>
> This is not subsidising decline: this is the Church continuing to be present where it is most needed, and where our Lord would most be found. A Church that has abandoned the poor and retreated to the gardens of the rich does not deserve the name 'Church' and will have earned the judgement that will surely come for it.

I only hope synod manages to arrive at a decision which allows parish churches to survive and stop the decline that I and my elderly friends have become all too aware.

Editorial Comment: This unexpected letter pinpointed the issue very clearly for those who are concerned about the survival of our parish churches, and the absolute need for those at the top in General Synod need to assure that the available financial resources are available for the main work of the Christian faith with each and every community, poor or rich, city or village.

Episcopal Appointments

When a police chief constable is selected for this top post, there must be some personal requirements which meet the basic demands for such a position of authority. There should be no doubt that his/her intelligence must be sound, that presentation of self is correct, that ability at public speaking is secure, and above all that they have a deep knowledge of police work, from walking the beat to police station administration, and have experience of all aspects of police commitments. They will need to be both sensitive to those who will be working under their orders and an awareness of public expectations. It is known by many in the police service that those who move up the ranks quickly are called 'fast trackers' and regarded somewhat cynically. It is generally understood that the person in control knows what it is like to stand before an angry mob, to be involved in a dangerous fast car chase, and suddenly have to face an armed opponent.

To become a head of a large school carries the same expectancies of having spent time at the coalface, or in this case the chalk or white board. Being a headmaster or mistress means administration, management, selecting the right staff, and holding their confidence. In the 1980s, some schools looked more to management and financial skills, and Cranleigh Public School in 1983 selected as their head a civil servant. The new man had limited experience with some teaching in Malawi during his gap year, his father had been a teacher. However, two years before his contract as headmaster ended, he was either politely asked to retire or he did it himself. There had been financial problems, and the intake of new pupils dropped to a serious level. It took the school four years before it became successful again. There are two factors here, the first being whether a civil servant knew how to run a school, and did he have the confidence of the staff and parents. It was significant that the board's later selection to take his place, was to select an experienced teacher who knew what classroom management was, the expectations of the teaching staff, and the demands of parents.

An army general or naval admiral is the peak of military responsibility, and according to both British and American guidelines they must have the following requirements. A sound education, undergo various assessments based on their experience, have at least two decades of service. In Britain, the initial commission of an officer is between ten to twelve years before he or she can look for further promotion. It takes years to reach this level and by the time the top post is achieved their occupancy maybe of a short duration with understandable exceptions in wartime. In the midst of war people are rapidly promoted from a sense of emergency, but even in peace they hold life and death in their hands and not least the safety of their country. Whether senior leading police officers, teachers, military, the most crucial factors are that their selection is based on their wide-ranging experience in their professions.

Bishops of the Church of England are currently appointed by a complex and convoluted system (which is currently under review), and the current system has worked since 1976. There are consultations with the diocese's cathedral dean, two archdeacons, General Synod members, members of the house of bishops, two or three from the house of clergy and house of laity, all done in the light of an assessment of the particular diocese's particular needs. Their findings are sent to the Crown Nominations Commission (until 2003 known as the Crown Appointments Commission) a smaller mixture of the components mentioned above, making fourteen voting members. The archbishop of the province normally chairs these meetings. It often meets in secret and the commission used to forward two names to the prime minister who made the final appointment. In recent years there has been only one known time when the prime minister (Margaret Thatcher) opposed a candidate whom she deemed to have left-leaning liberal views. Once the candidate has accepted the offer the monarch is informed. It has also been drawn to our attention that in regard to the Crown Nominations Commission, Gordon Brown when prime minister changed the system so that the CNC nominated the name of the preferred candidate to the prime minister, who submits it to the monarch for approval. Once approved, the appointment is announced by 10 Downing Street. The CNC can vote for a second name as a 'spare', but they must also get over the two-thirds majority of the votes.

In times past it used to be an ongoing joke that if one wanted to aspire to becoming a bishop it was necessary to have been an Oxbridge graduate. To 'aspire' to be a bishop ought not to be the ambition for any ordained deacon or priest, because it is a vocation and not a career post. All priests hold deacon's orders, and all bishops remain priests and deacons. It is not a rank but a calling. All newly ordained clergy are curates in a parish, and forty to fifty years ago they usually had two 'titles', (today a curacy can be a matter of a few years or even months), meaning two curacies which could extend over four to six years, if not more. Eventually the curate is given an incumbency as either a vicar, or rector, and more recently the priest in charge, for some the first parish can be a lifelong experience, for others just a few years as various forms of chaplaincies can often attract attention.

For the editors of this project, and like many others who are worried about the future of the traditional parish system, which is the bedrock of the Christian faith in every community, there have been concerns that not all bishops are switched on to the critical importance of the parish system. A police chief constable would know how important his officer on the beat is, and that those in patrol cars are essential, the headteacher that his staff educate and care for their pupils, and a military general knows that his foot soldiers are critical despite developing technology, all based on wide early life experiences. In seeing the development of new posts attached to diocesan offices and the erosion of parishes the question, embarrassing as it is, must be asked how far the current bishops have had personal parish experience.

A recent Crockford's directory was explored and out of thirty-eight diocesan bishops (there were several vacancies) 13 per cent had no parish experience, 65 per cent had less than ten years as an incumbent, those who served over a decade amounted to 34 per cent, and just one who served for over two decades which amounted to less than 3 per cent. This indicated that the vast majority had either no experience or extremely limited first-hand parish experience. Bishops may have intelligence, wisdom, a sound Christian spirituality, so may airline pilots, but they also need to know the essential navigational aids, which for bishops must be the work of the parishes. Any pilot who cannot find the landing place, as bright, as pleasant and educated as he or she may be, becomes a possible disaster. The parishes are just as critical in Church life as the knowledge of landing places are for a pilot, and if the parishes disappear the loss would be momentous in terms not just of the Church of England, but the Christian faith.

Over the last few decades parish clergy have lost the rights of freehold, the expression interregnum has been replaced by vacancy, the old-fashioned titles of rector and vicar are giving way to priests-in-charge, and the term Church management is becoming more the focal point. It is understood that as one era gives way to the next in terms of development and changes, which have to be accepted, there should also be an awareness when the changes become retrogressive. Christ is the foundation stone, and in the Church of England the parish system has been built on this belief. Taking Christ into every local community is the work of the parish, and in the growing centralisation of Church development of plans and progress the parish system is slowly fading, and although many bishops are rightly concerned about this problem, it seems that not all of them have the necessary experience of having worked in the parish for a learning curve to be embedded. In the army it is noted that at least twenty years of base experience is required before making the rank of a general, but in this survey only one bishop had such experience at parish level.

Freehold Independence or Controlled Employees?

In the reporting of the February 2025 General Synod, the possibility of clergy being regarded as 'employees' dominated much of the news. This appeared to many as the end-result of what has been happening over the last few decades when parish priests who felt a calling, a vocation to serve God, could do so because they were trusted. Their work and Christian conscience were generally accepted, and they were not seen as employees of a centralised management office. There have been occasional mishaps, but a vocation is seen as a calling by God, not a post designated by some head office. The ramifications of this latest development are deep and complex, and as an immediate response the editors asked one of the team with his lifelong experience to express his personal views.

When I was very young my father was the incumbent of three villages in Somerset. Apparently, it was quite a talking point at the time that he had three villages to look after. People thought it was too much for one man. He was always busy, and the bishop must have been concerned because he put his name forward for one of the free holidays that Billy Butlin, the holiday camp boss, used to donate for clergy use. My middle-class grandparents were aghast at the idea of us going to a holiday camp, but my brothers and I had a 'whale of a time'.

The rectory where we lived had three fields attached to it, which were Glebe land. The rent from them was part of my father's stipend. It was a different world. Those parishes are now part of a group of six and they are in a vacancy, their former house for a duty priest having been sold some time ago. Being a parish priest in those days, the 1940s, was a complete way of life. The incumbent was involved in every level of parish and village life. The parish priest was secure in his living because he had the freehold. In theory he could preach the gospel in whatever way he thought fit, 'in season and out of season'. He could criticise the bishop if he wanted to, and who could do nothing about it being obliged to accept this, because the freehold gave the parish priest independence and security. It was replaced in 2011 by common tenure whereby the parish priest became an 'office holder'. In these days, in some dioceses, parish priests are initially being appointed on a three-year interim basis, with no guarantee that the post will become permanent.

Some might see these changes as a serious erosion of the status of the parish priest, with the bishops gathering more and more power to themselves. It has occurred at the same time that the Church has been placing more emphasis on management. Recently the Archbishop of York has suggested that parish clergy should become employees. It could be argued that the archbishop's suggestion is the final stage of this process, or it might be presented that these changes are necessary to create more flexibility and better oversight of the clergy. Common tenure has the advantage of putting all parish clergy on the same basis together with clergy on general licences.

We have seen in recent times that freehold can be an obstacle in cases of clergy discipline. In the past it has also caused problems with pastoral reorganisation, when a priest with freehold refuses to cooperate with suggested change. One can understand the frustration of bishops when sometimes they have to deal with an uncooperative, incompetent or an idle priest who they cannot remove.

The real question is about responsibility. I was a parish priest myself in three different benefices for over thirty years before retirement and had the freehold all that time, with 'all the rights, benefits and appurtenances'. I might add that I never really discovered what an appurtenance was! I do not recall thinking about my freehold all that much, although I am sure that it did give an underlying sense of security. The more important thing it conferred was a sense of responsibility. The parish was yours to develop or 'muck up'. On reflection it was quite a sobering thought.

Common tenure does seem to strike a good balance between the preserving the rights and responsibilities of parish clergy and to maintain their independence while allowing more flexibility. The Archbishop of York's suggestion would completely change things. One of the distinctive things about parish clergy is that they are not employees. They are committed to doing their work in their own way. They are not subject to supervision by their bishop in the work they do, although they may seek guidance if they wish. In fact, bishops are generally ill-equipped to micro-manage parishes anyway, because they cannot know the local situation as well as the parish priest. If parish clergy were employees there would need to be a list of the tasks and functions which they are supposed to perform. Parish ministry cannot be like this. Ideally it is seen as a way of life, which may involve all sort of things that cannot be anticipated. The bishop has pastoral oversight of the diocese, but this is delegated to the incumbent when he or she is instituted or licenced. The crucial words when that happens are, 'Receive this charge which is both yours and mine', delivered when the deed of institution or licence is handed to the priest. Thereafter the incumbent is expected and trusted to get on with the task in hand. The bishop is there as their 'Father in God', not as their project manager.

If parish clergy were to become employees there would have to be some form of job description. It would need to contain a list of the things the priest was supposed to do. This would be an extremely difficult thing to produce since the task varies from parish to parish and changes from time to time. The strength of the local parish priest, ideally living in the benefice, is that they will know what needs to be done and how to manage the tasks. This is of course idealistic, but the principle remains sound. It should also be noted that a description could actually have a negative effect, and a priest might limit him or herself simply to the tasks described and never do anything beyond them, or work in an imaginative and creative way.

It would certainly be easier for bishops to dismiss clergy if they were employees. This is one of the current Archbishop of York's objectives, but what criteria would be used beyond the obvious aspects like criminal or scandalous behaviour? Would it be possible to sack an incumbent for obstructing pastoral reorganisation in some way? It is possible to imagine a situation where the bishop sincerely believed that 'parish A' ought to be joined up with 'parish B', but there was an existing incumbent in one of the parishes, who refused to cooperate. He or she might know the local history better and recognise that there were deeply held local problems between the two parishes, and that they would never work together. Would it be possible to dismiss an incumbent who found himself or herself in this position?

In the end what matters is the parish. If the incumbent were an employee, would they be able to object to changing the relationship with the parish. There is nothing wrong with being an employee in itself. After all, most people work as employees of someone else, and clergy should not expect privileged treatment, but the question is how it impacts on the parish. At present parish clergy are not generally seen as a bishop's local agents, but as occupants of a unique place in their local community. Surprisingly there is still a great deal of good will towards someone wearing a dog collar, but this might not continue if the person wearing it was seen as working for a distant Church dignitary.

Naturally this issue does not arise so much in the case of self-supporting ministers and part-time ones, but surely, we should assume that there will always be a need for a core of full-time clergy, that is well trained priests with highly developed pastoral skills, living amongst the people they serve. The present writer is involved in helping a possible ordinand through the long process of discernment now used. In the guidance notes he has been given the word 'vocation' does not seem to appear.

Ordination Training

Editor: Andrew Sangster

There has been considerable discussion not just about the lack of ordained clergy but the way the training has changed, and like all groups the editors of this project have mixed views. Three of the editors went through the old system when there was a variety of colleges one could attend, and one editor was trained in a regional course. This article has been left to the last moment while we have mulled the issues over. Until a few years ago this editor felt somewhat critical of what he called part-time training, but as the years have passed there has been a change of mind as he met new clergy trained under the so-called part-time systems and has been very impressed by these priests.

In the old system this editor went to King's College London, took a BD Honours degree, with a special interest in text and canon, studying Greek and Hebrew. The course covered, Church history, comparative religions, moral philosophy, doctrine and many other areas. The course was taken not just by ordinands and was quite difficult as we were plunged into Greek and Hebrew in the first term, and many dropped out. After three years and a degree in divinity it was off to St Boniface College, Warminster for one year. This consisted of lectures and talks on belief, obedience, the nature of prayer. It included preparing sermons which were not just academic diatribes, of listening to visiting parish priests helping to take services in local churches, and as groups visiting parishes across the UK for a week at a time. The college naturally involved a routine of services from the early hours to late night compline, with time set aside for meditation. There were well over sixty there, and one was aged about thirty and known as 'grandad' as most were in their early twenties. The college closed in 1969 and Kingsmen went to St Augustine's College in Canterbury. St Boniface became a public school, but once a year for just short of fifty years a retreat was held for those who had once attended.

The old college, despite its long history was apparently closed for financial reasons. This way of training was regarded as the norm, but one by one many such theological colleges were beginning to close, notably

Kelham which had a good reputation. For older clergy this form of ordination was the way forward, but by the 1980s appeared to be faltering. It is impossible for us, 'the uninformed', to know whether it was because of lack of ordinands or financial reasons. A few of us remain, but many men and women of wider experience than very young men are today offering themselves to the calling. They go through the various courses organised in different parts of the UK, and according to some responses noted in this project, some courses were well-known and praised, others less so.

As noted earlier this writer had a degree of scepticism about the new system, but having met and worked with men and women from these courses there has been a change of mind, because their calling and quality is unquestionable. Some may disagree with this viewpoint which is why all editors have been asked to express their views.

Editor: Simon Wright

These comments about clergy training come from one who has spent almost his entire ministry, from 1968 until 2010, as a parish priest, with the exception of five years spent as director of ordinands in the diocese of York, from 1979 until 1984. During that time, I had six curates, all of whom came as deacons. They were all from different colleges and courses. Nevertheless, since retiring, I have had the chance to observe those clergy more recently trained.

My first observation is that the newly ordained who came to work with me were pretty well trained and prepared academically and open to further practical or pastoral training. I found no difference between those trained on courses and those trained in colleges.

However, in more recent years I have become quite concerned about the training the recently ordained seemed to have received. Some do not seem to have much idea of biblical criticism, and they do not seem to have been given the tools to approach the scriptures in a methodical and questioning way. Also, I have noticed a lack of knowledge of Church history or an understanding of why it is helpful or important.

My greatest concern is for what used to be called post-ordination training. The first few years in holy orders are a crucial and formative time, and the training incumbent was entrusted with the huge responsibility of supervising this continued study. Nowadays many clergy serve their curacies as self-supporting ministers, which means that with the best will in the world, there is little time for this sort of training. Also, the newly ordained seem to be moved on to posts where they have sole responsibility after only a short period, such as only two years or even less. This is a huge mistake and a great loss to the Church.

Those early years are a time for major adjustments and the learning of new skills. Whatever the pre-ordination experience, a curate might have, they need to learn to adapt it and integrate it into their work as an ordained minister. The biggest change is that they find themselves working almost exclusively with volunteers rather than employees or professional colleagues. It is very different experience, and relationships have to develop accordingly.

Ideally those early years are a time for the newly ordained to work out how their own ministry is developing, and where their strengths and weaknesses are. The method most training clergy would employ was to get the newly ordained curate to shadow them for their first year and then pass on more and more responsibility. During this period hopefully skills would be passed on and developed.

Some may think it odd to talk about skills in this context, but a good parish priest is a highly skilled person. One of their skills has already been implied in the issue of working with volunteers. Sometimes this involves patience, courtesy, charity, and is often quite hard. Another skill involves the application of theory to practice. For example, the minister may have a dreadful time at a PCC meeting, but he still needs to remember he is working within the body of Christ.

There are many skills required in conducting worship well. For example, some do not seem to know the difference between addressing the congregation, addressing almighty God, and addressing God on behalf of the congregation. Voice levels and physical position come into this. It should be noted that worship is different for the ordained person. If they are responsible for leading it, they may be distracted by its mechanics, worrying, for example, that the organist knows that we are leaving out the starred verses in the next hymn. They need to find a way to make such concerns part of their own offering of worship. Many communication skills are helpful in all sorts of situations, chairing meetings, leading groups, marriage preparation and so on. Obviously preaching skills are vital.

There is quite a lot about parish visiting in this book and it certainly requires some skills. Putting people at ease, looking for conversation starters, such as immaculate gardens or lots of pictures of dogs around the house. Evidence of a wider family may be observed if there are such photos around the house. Crucially visiting clergy need to avoid leading any conversation and let people speak for themselves. These are just examples of some of the practical skills a newly ordained minister should be given time and help in developing in their early years in ministry.

Sadly, there is evidence that some clergy have not had time or opportunity for this preparation, and it can easily result in misunderstandings and problems later. Investment in this kind of training would later pay major dividends. We live in a complex and sometimes unsympathetic world and clergy need to be better trained now than in the past.

Editor: Maurice Keys

As a non-ordained person, I respond to the question of ordination training from that of a person on the outside looking in, at essentially the final product. The selected candidate, who has put themselves through the selection training, the interview process and the rigorous study put to those who feel a calling to be a clerk in holy orders.

From my understanding of the process of ordination training it takes place over a period of time allowing candidates to fully consider if they feel they are the most appropriate person with their life and faith skills, who are robust and honest enough to hear God's calling in their life, and they respond to that calling in the way they can make a difference. Basic requirements to me would seem to be a grounding in the understanding in the faith that we profess, being able to share that faith and being able to lead by way of Christian example.

From my career in the secular world, I have been fortunate enough to have sat on both sides of the table at interviews as an interviewer and an interviewee. That experience has taught me a great deal about people and the psychology of people in how and why they relate. A well-qualified candidate might well interview poorly for an unknown reason on the day of interview, while a less able candidate may have the gift of the gab and be able to sell themselves into a position beyond their capabilities.

Sometimes people's life experiences are of much more value than academic qualifications. For example, I know of someone who works as a technician at a very sophisticated level, who works with others who are far better qualified academically, yet because they only have the academic and not the practical experience, they rely on him to resolve many of their issues. Nevertheless, one would need to look beyond one's qualifications, perhaps to their faith story their life experiences and aspirations.

I note another of our contributors to this edition comments on the closing of theological colleges and raises concerns about the way that the education and training have changed. Should this be a concern for the future of our Church I ask myself? In our current Anglican communion, the Church is formed over strands ranging from high Anglo-Catholic to middle of the road to evangelical. So, with the closing of some of those training establishments I ask myself does not the rich choices of colleges diminish the training if less are available? I would personally hate to think that through economic measures the opportunities afforded to those who would wish to present themselves to holy orders might be diminished through lack of opportunities. For each candidate would have their own life story and their own faith comfort zone. I would not want to see a Henry Ford style of production line of clergy where all clergy are produced in a stereotype, and all come out the same. To me, faith is a very individual and personal issue and this needs to be reflected in the way that candidates are selected and trained, not only in the tradition with which they are most familiar, but in order that they can operate in the areas of the Church they are most comfortable, so that they can serve at their optimum best.

By way of an aside, I recall on one occasion when a non-church going member of the public decided to write to a parish to enquire about a business matter. Not knowing to whom they should address the letter they simply addressed it to the chief executive of the parish of … This to me shows that ordained clergy in post have to perform a number of roles which could be seen in the secular world under a number of different descriptions i.e. diplomat, teacher, confidant, finance manager, entertainer, tea maker, technician and many others. So surely, the ordination training given should reflect of all of those skills required for this calling to make the most efficient and effective candidates for those posts.

So, whilst learning Hebrew and Greek for the average clergy in post how useful is that skill on a daily basis? In an academic environment it may well form an essential part of the curriculum and be learnt, translated and debated on but just how useful is it in the world outside academia? If we think about this going forward, if a parish were to consider setting up an alpha group or similar teaching resource to a group of new Christians in a modern-day inner-city estate how many of them would relate to ancient Greek and Hebrew. Might instead the youth of today relate better to a short Facebook, Twitter or other electronic exchanges in which to engage. For just consider today how we relate to our nearest and dearest to explain something to them.

I also note that one of our correspondents noted the reduction in understanding and educational ability for new candidates, but surely this problem stems from earlier in the candidate's education. Thinking back to my school days the religious instruction classes provided in the 1960s and 1970s was primarily done on the basis of a Christian teaching. Our modern teaching methods in contrast teach religious instruction or whatever one wants to call it in as a multi-faith experience. In doing so, whilst giving a brief overview of alternative beliefs and faiths it does rather dilute the specific Christian teaching that would have been provided in my youth. By this the candidates of today would have received less Christian teaching than their forebears of some forty or more years earlier.

One is conscious that we all need to move with the times, but we also need to provide a ministry in training that lives in the modern world, but it is essentially one that can produce clerks in holy orders who are sufficiently accessible to all.

Editor: Peter Doll

After a recent Sunday service, I met a young visitor from the Netherlands who, it turned out, was preparing for ministry in the Dutch Reformed Church. I asked whether, as I found to be typical of other Protestant churches in Europe, he was still expected to learn the three classical languages, Hebrew, Greek and Latin, as integral to his formation. He said he was, and that an ability to read scripture in its original languages was seen as fundamental to being a minister of the word. What a contrast, I reflected, to the Church of England, where learning any of these languages, much less all of them, is now the exception rather than the rule.

One of the other contributors in this section has raised the question of just how practically useful knowledge of Hebrew and Greek would be in a priest's day-to-day ministry. While I would assume that scriptural engagement should always inform a priest's teaching and preaching, the issue as I see it is much larger, much more than a question of what would be useful to running a parish. It is a question of perspective: of whether the Church is simply an organisation that here and now offers worship and pastoral care, runs programmes, and advertises itself to the wider world via social media; or whether it is fundamentally the body of Christ, its members being among the children of Abraham, Isaac and Jacob, and part of a community of faith that encompasses past, present, and future, that embraces people of every race and tongue. If our vision of the Church is confined to what happens to seem relevant or useful to us now, then we will lose any sense of the vast dimensions of the fellowship to which we belong and to which we are accountable. Henry Chadwick, one of the greatest scholars of the twentieth century, a priest and ecumenist, reminded the General Synod in 1988, 'Nothing is sadder than someone who has lost his memory, and the Church which has lost its memory is in the same state of senility.' The Church of England has not heeded his warning; loss of memory has become our way of life.

I came to theological college as what Andrew Sangster's generation would have called a 'grandad', beginning just after my thirtieth birthday. In my generation, many of us came to ordination formation in our thirties, after we'd had some experience of life and work 'in the world'.

An American by birth, I did my first degree in the United States, worked for two years in Wall Street, gained a doctorate in modern history from Oxford, and then worked as a librarian. Because of my age, I had to get permission to have three years in theological college rather than two, in order to do a theological degree, which was granted on the basis of potential to become a theological educator. I mention this since my point of view presupposes a valuing of the importance of academic theological formation. There is an operating assumption that such a pattern will not be suitable for every ordinand; I can only say that residential training had a decisive impact on my understanding of ministry and its foundational disciplines; with the theology degree, I was given the tools I needed to enrich my historical studies within a theological and ecclesial context and understand my day-to-day ministry within God's eternal revelation of himself.

At the same time, doing theology in the academic context of a university alerted me to the danger of relying exclusively on the values of the academy. The university wants to treat theology like any other subject, to be studied objectively and dispassionately, without any regard to belief in the truth of God. As Eric Mascall pointed out, the academic attitude 'finds it interesting to investigate why men thought as they did about God but is unconcerned with whether [what] they thought about him is true or false'. For me, this attitude was epitomised in biblical studies, which I enjoyed as an intellectual discipline combining languages, literature, and history, but which discouraged me from considering either the truth of God or whether the Old and New Testaments were integral parts of the same whole. The corrective came to me in Patristic studies on the origins of doctrine. There, taught by a brilliant and inspiring Roman Catholic priest, I discovered the wonderful world of typological interpretation, which made Scripture come alive to me in a way that nothing else ever has.

Academic training was insufficient in itself to prepare for ministry; it was essential for me that it was offered in the context of a residential praying community which inculcated in me the discipline of the daily office which, with the Eucharist, is the bedrock of ministry, and which nurtured the love of God and the love of Scripture within me and sustained me in ministry ever since. Theology divorced from prayer becomes an exercise in mental gymnastics rather than a search for truth. Ministry unfounded in prayer becomes a self-offering from the shallow pool of my own limited generosity and insight rather than from the limitless grace and generosity of God. I learned to prize the monastic tradition's intimate joining of prayer and study, expressed in the title of Dom Jean Leclercq's classic book, *The Love of Learning and the Desire for God*, which is learning in order to 'know' God, rather than to 'know about' him.

The number of ordinands who will have the opportunity to experience residential formation is becoming fewer and fewer. Will residential colleges ultimately disappear entirely, with part-time courses the only option? Such obsolescence marks the devaluing of parish ministry as a way of life marked by a commitment to daily public prayer and study alongside pastoral ministry and service. The Church of England's growing memory loss is taking the form of a rejection of what historically was its pride and strength, parochial ministry which was not narrowly Church of England but knew itself to be both deeply rooted in its local community and also a constituent part of the universal Church, accountable to fellow members of the body of Christ across time and space.

Editor: Christopher Ellis

I trained for ordination on the Eastern Region Ministry Course (ERMC), part of the Cambridge Theological Federation which moderates the training of all the residential Theological Colleges in Cambridge as well as the part-time course. I do not remember much conversation with the DDO about options for training and it seemed to be assumed that as a married man with a mortgage, wife and children the part-time course was the obvious choice. I do at times reflect on what I may have missed out on by not studying full-time and living in a collegiate setting, but on balance I feel fortunate to have taken the path I did. Comment is sometimes made that the course is an easier, less rigorous form of training which I would firmly refute. The course covered biblical studies, hermeneutics, Church history, doctrine, ethics, preaching etc and in my day you were allocated a local tutor with whom you had weekly tutorials supplemented by regular weekend residentials and summer schools. Juggling the study alongside a demanding full-time job, family life and Church life was a constant challenge, and I believe an excellent preparation for the rigours of ministry and its need for time-management and the acceptance that doing your best with the time available rather than expecting perfection was a life skill well learned.

When I was accepted for the course, I had an interview with the vice-principal, and I remember her advice very clearly which was to enter the training with 'roots down and walls down'. In other words, be confident in who you are and your churchmanship, but be open to the great variety of theological views and liturgical practice you will encounter. Most of the ordinands were Church of England, but we also had Methodists and United Reform candidates alongside us. This brought a great depth to the lectures and lively discussions in the bar in the evenings on residentials! Within the Church of England fraternity, we had all points on the spectrum from very traditional Anglo-Catholics to conservative Evangelicals and we all managed to happily co-exist, learning from each other along the way. I know that critics suggest that regional courses, by their all-encompassing nature, produce middle of the road Anglicans with poor biblical knowledge which upsets the evangelicals and a lack of liturgical integrity which offends the Anglo-Catholics, but my experience was that most candidates emerged with a much clearer understanding of their own churchmanship and a greater perception of other views than traditional colleges probably encourage. Whilst we hear clergy being referred to as 'a Mirfield man' or a 'Westcott woman' I have never been labelled as a 'regional course rector', and I consider that a positive rather than a negative thing.

When I began the course, I was fortunate to do so after some previous theological study which had earned me some university credits and enabled me to graduate with a BA (Hons) degree in Christian Theology rather than the certificate or diploma with which most students emerge. I have always been grateful for the opportunity to study to degree level as far fewer clergy have theology degrees than was previously the case, and a degree suggests a depth of study and knowledge which is perhaps still necessary for clergy in their leadership role.

I served my curacy in a large parish where there was ample opportunity to develop the necessary skills required in what is still a unique professional role. I had great freedom and the relationship with my training incumbent was key to my development; he was trusted to train me and to make the decision on how prepared I was to move on to my first incumbency. Having trained curates myself in recent years, it is a very different situation with the role of the training incumbent being surpassed by the DDO and curates now spending far too much time creating portfolios and gathering 'evidence' of their learning. This takes too much time in what is already a shortened period of curacy to previous generations, and I fear that it produces academically able but not necessarily pastorally gifted clergy.

In the modern world and Church with more mature individuals coming forward for ordination, I believe regional courses offer a more flexible training model than the traditional college system and can produce ordinands with a greater understanding of the variety and complexity of ministry within the Church of England. The quality of the priest that emerges is dependent on the application of the student rather than the context or location of the lectures.

Final Observations: Among the editors there were variety of different opinions, not in a divisive sense but mainly reflecting our own pasts and offering some personal insights. If a group of people are advised to find a way up a steep and difficult hill, we must listen to what is the best approach. For some it may take longer to make it because they were shown a long safe path, but which could take a longer time. Others may take a craggy route with a few dangers because it may involve climbing but could be quicker. Once the destination is completed it is considered a success, and the choice of routes will be up for discussion once the hilltop is reached. For most people this is irrelevant once the journey is done, and we sit together as a team ready to start working together. The only reason this aspect was considered by the project team was because often the changes in ordination training were noted, sometimes quite critically. It could be argued that in all routes there are flaws and dangers but reaching the top of the hill is a sure sign that a person called to be a deacon or priest had been 'called' by God, end of matter.

Chapter One

Views of Clergy Still in Post

As with other chapters, the contributors are placed in the order in which they arrived.

Introduction

Parish Priests who are currently serving all have various backgrounds, some have been in post for nearly forty years, and some have just started their first incumbency. Some serve in Anglo-Catholic churches, some within the evangelical wing and others in what is often called the middle of the road parishes. It once used to be known as High, Low, and Middle-of the Road often jokingly asked where one was on the candle, at the top, the bottom or halfway. Some serve in vast rural areas, some in small and large towns, and other in cities which can range from historically interesting centres to major industrial areas. The life may be different, but the fundamentals are the same, to lead the worship, to care for the congregation, to be known in the parish generally as the parish priest who visits those who need attention and love, and others who have expressed some interest in the faith. The parish priest is expected to baptise the new-born, officiate at marriages, and conduct funerals either in the Church or the crematorium. From these efforts it often happens that the congregation will grow. The parish priest whether he/she wants to be, becomes a public figure. They are expected to visit the sick, and to attend those who are dying when the medical profession has stood back, and most family members keep a discreet distance. They are in place to care for any and all within their parish boundaries. The Church considers this as God's work, as the worship of God takes place in the parish church, and by visiting the love of God is felt. Many parish priests feel it is a privilege to be involved in so many households whether it be the joy of baptising and marriage, as well as the more painful assistance offered at funerals, being with parishioners at the best and the worse times of their life. The old gibe that a parish priest only works one day a week is known by most to be nonsense, and many only have one day off a week, and that can easily be wrecked by a sudden funeral call which takes priority. Sometimes they have the assistance of a training curate, or a retired priest who has moved into the parish. They may have worship lay assistants, or a reader, and married priests often have a wife or husband who not only supports at home but can be a welcome and beneficial help in the parish, either in the Church, social functions, fetes, or even at a personal level to someone who needs to speak outside the box.

As the years have passed most parish priests are conscious that they must have a good treasurer and or finance committee as the parish share has escalated, and there is a growing concern that the congregation tends to be older people, and fewer are attending worship, which some find depressing. Many are conscious they are now priests-in-charge and no longer have the traditional freehold, which means they are even more under the authority of the bishop. The older style of freehold incumbency meant the priest could disagree with the bishop's request or even opinions, but as a priest-in-charge must tread with more care. As such, it was no surprise that serving clergy when asked to offer their opinions for this project-effort either politely refused while expressing sympathy, while others asked to remain totally anonymous, one, and only one, explaining she was anticipating some form of 'promotion'. In their replies a few explained why they preferred to remain unknown, and all this must be respected.

Rt Revd. Geoff Annas

This welcome contribution came from a bishop who offers his name and his experience in the opening section.

I am the Rt Revd. Geoff Annas, ordained 1983 diocese of Southwark and served as curate and my first post was in an Urban Priority Area

(UPA) Parish in Central London. I moved to another UPA Parish in Southampton (diocese of Winchester) and served there for sixteen years. I was Bishop of Stafford from 2010 until retirement at the end of 2019. I am now Honourable Assistant Bishop in diocese of Winchester (served as Acting Bishop of Southampton during 2024). I have experience of ministry across the traditions but feel most comfortable in a modern Catholic to 'middle of the road' setting which moulds my views, and my wish for a totally inclusive Church. However, I value and respect those who hold an alternative understanding.

Following a social science degree I gained a post graduate diploma in Social Work and was with Surrey County Council for ten years before going to Salisbury and Wells Theological College, where I was a residential student for three years. I found living in The Close in Salisbury quite claustrophobic, and so on the advice of the College Principal found part-time work in an Adolescent Assessment Centre which I did alongside my Theology Degree and which I found enhanced my studies. The young people were constantly interested and asking questions about faith.

A six-week parish placement in the College's Link Parish at the Elephant and Castle was both liberating and life-changing, and I was delighted when I was invited to join that parish for my Curacy. I arrived at the time of the Brixton Riots, and so from the start had an awareness of the importance of the parish church as being a centre for the whole community, especially at times of difficulty and challenge. As a curate I was living in a flat on the twelfth floor of a block of flats in one of three large estates in the parish. I always wore my dog collar and if going to a funeral would walk through the streets in my cassock, so I quickly became known as 'one of the Fathers' at St Matthew's. This opened so many doors for me and enabled me to become involved with many of the groups meeting in the community including the schools. Within the community there was respect for the Church built up over many years of faithful service. Those who rarely attended Sunday worship felt comfortable about coming into the building for the key moments in their lives.

I found that I had a representative role supporting those who found it difficult to relate to 'authority'. Most of those in the parish were not enjoying the benefits of Mrs Thatcher's Britain, and I developed a particular role in working with the homeless and those who were 'squatters'. We also had a special ministry to the young people on the Estates and delivering the Church Newspaper every month which helped with building a sense of community as well as enabling us to encounter all kinds of people.

I think my training Parish was truly inclusive, and we worked closely with the other Christian denominations and were gradually building inter-faith links. We were also blessed with a wonderful laity for whom 'living out their faith' was just the natural thing to do and who taught me far more than any post ordination training courses (even though in Southwark these were exceptionally good). Reflecting now I can genuinely say that my experiences during my four years of curacy have shaped my entire ministry. I believe that everything that happens to us, for good or ill, can be and is used by God, and I am certainly grateful for that formative part of my own spiritual journey. I feel equally grateful for all that has happened in the parishes where I have been called to serve. I use these words deliberately because I believe a sense of 'calling' is essential for every form of ministry. It has been my experience that believing you are doing what God wants you to do, gets you through the toughest of challenges.

At the end of the curacy, I went as vicar to The Old Kent Road and served in a parish that incorporated half of the Aylesbury Estate, later to be used by Tony Blair as the setting for his first 'Things Can Only Get Better' speech as he celebrated his election as prime minister. Here there were not the firm foundations I had enjoyed at the Elephant and Castle. I was appointed at the end of a six-year vacancy and both the previous two vicars had been forced to leave after very short periods of ministry because of the pressures. There was a regular congregation of just six people and the building was dominated by a youth club and a social club which had pushed the worship area into a small and insignificant space. Most of the local community did not even know this was a Church!

However, I came to understand that starting from such a 'low base' was actually quite a blessing because not having to maintain a status quo, all I could see was potential and possibility. Gradually we began to attract some wonderful people from the Parish homes to the Church (I rang the Church bell for the first time in years and Joyce (later a dedicated member of the Church) told me she heard it and just decided to come, and by the time we moved on, eight years later, we had a regular weekly congregation of 60. Both the youth club and social club were flourishing and most important of all they shared a refurbished building that provided a worship space that was so attractive we were actually holding weddings for the first time in years. The people in the local community once again regarded St Christopher's as 'their' Church and knew that if they visited, they would be welcome. They also knew that the 'Church' would come to them if they needed help and support of any kind. This was also the way people regarded another St Christopher's – this one in Southampton – where I had the privilege of serving for sixteen years.

I realise that I have been exceptionally blessed in serving in such wonderful parishes where, as noted here certain characteristics were essential:

a. There is a clear geographical boundary.
b. The population in each was around 10,000 but contained within a very small area which enabled me to walk around the Parish, meeting the people and being known by them.
c. Challenging social issues enable the local parish church to make a positive contribution to people's well-being and through this engagement people come to know the love of God.
d. Each contained schools that welcomed local Church involvement.
e. I was able to be part of lively and supportive clergy chapters with colleagues who were working in similar settings and understood the demands and joys of ministry in the UPA. We were not from the same traditions yet maintained good relationships even when the National Church and General Synod were battling with the issues of the day – the re-marriage of divorcees in Church and of course the ordination of women to the Priesthood and Episcopate.
f. Bishops and archdeacons who were supportive and who understood because of their own personal experience of being parish priests.

Knowing they were there 24/7 to help you, meant that in reality I very rarely needed to call upon them, but annual ministry reviews were helpful – not least because they focused on me and the needs of my family as much as what was happening in the Church and community.

g. I was able to work alongside (and come to both understand and value) non-parochial forms of ministry and especially chaplaincy. My main encounters were with those in hospital, school and prison chaplaincy, but as a bishop I enjoyed working with others – not least those chaplains working with the police and armed services. I was able to offer theatre chaplaincy alongside my Parish ministry.
h. Within society there was still a good percentage of people who knew something about Jesus and that 'belief in God' was a good thing – even if you did not go to Church!

I am very sad about the present state of the Church of England, and as I approach the end of my ministry it is very different from how I envisaged it would be when I was ordained. But then – being totally honest, England (and indeed the world) is not as I envisaged it would be. As a young person I grew up in a post-world war setting where Prime Minister Harold Macmillan could proclaim that we had 'never had it so good' and was not contradicted. The 1960s and 70s were full of hope and optimism, and when I worked in the UPA parishes it was within the context of the 'Faith In The City' report, and the assumption that all that was wrong with society could be put right, and that everyone would eventually have a decent home, good medical care, an education that would enable them to have work and that individuals would feel valued and part of a larger community. It was also with the hope that despite the Cold War there would eventually be peace on earth.

Put even more simply, I saw my role as a priest as trying to bring others to know the love of Jesus through prayerfully living out the Christian Faith as we have it in the Gospels, and I felt sure that in doing so God's kingdom would continue to be established. Frankly, at times trying to put this into practice was both demanding and hard work, but I felt valued by the people I tried to serve and the Church 'hierarchy'. Above all, I had a sense of the Spirit going before me, supporting and enabling my ministry.

This basic belief is still at the heart of all I do, but I personally think the Church of England as a whole, had never envisaged the dramatic changes that would come in the twenty-first century. The technological revolution and especially the grip of social media, the pace of climate change, multi-culturalism and multi-faith communities have resulted in the transformation of the Second Elizabethan Age, being as great as those of the Victorian Age, and the impact on the life of the Church in England has been just as dramatic.

We know that God has been faithful and certainly the Christian Church has changed and developed continually since the time of Jesus, and I have no doubt will continue to do so. My personal hope is that our Church leaders and General Synod will have the courage to tackle the issues that are generating such 'bad press' in our days and enable the Church of England to move on, and once again be focused on prayer and service and enable our churches to be places where people will want to belong. Mental health statistics alone indicate the need for people to rediscover a sense of 'belonging' and for me, the Church has always offered this opportunity for fellowship with God and with one another.

I believe that interest in the faith is as great today as it has ever been, but that organised religion has become a barrier for people rather than a way to God. I just rejoice that it is God who takes the initiative and comes to find us, and I am certain however faithless we may be, God will fashion a Church fit for out times.

Editorial Comment: This interesting contribution from a bishop offers a glimmer of hope, not least in reminding us of God, the impetus for us and our work. Working in an urban deprived area, which this editor did once, demands hard work, overcoming a degree of gloom, but finding mission and hope. His comments on his first curacy and how important it was for his overall ministry will ring bells for many, especially given that because of clergy shortages some curacies are short in duration. When he wrote 'those who rarely attended Sunday worship felt comfortable about coming into the building for the key moments in their lives', he underlines a major issue that non-church goers still turn to the parish church for the great family celebrations of marriage and baptism, and also the times of deep sadness for funerals. This is a key point for the parish's future.

In places his experience taught him to almost have to start from scratch, and ringing the church bell rang many other bells, reminding parishioners it was 'their church'. He pointed out the size of a parish is important and as with many other contributors the part the parish clergy play, especially in schools. He also makes the pertinent point we live in a changing world, not it might be noted, changing for the better with the usual worldwide political problems, the dangers of climate change, but his hope in God is evident and for all of us appropriate and relevant. This bishop's experience is urban based and important but does not reflect many of the problems in the vast rural areas of growing benefices, churches closing, shortage of clergy, but he points out the importance of the sense of community the parish can inspire. He wrote that 'my personal hope is that our Church leaders and General Synod will have the courage to tackle the issues that are generating such 'bad press' in our days and enable the Church of England to move on', which is the *raison d'être* of this project, not to result in bad press but to be heard. This contributor's sense of hope is critical for all of us, which is why this project was launched in the first place as part of a navigation scheme, and by asking committed people for their views so they may be heard within our community of faith.

Anonymous

I was ordained deacon in August 2020, priested 2021 but I would rather not be identified. I was trained on a regional course, the ERMC. This was a part-time process. I worked full time in the week and attended classes online once a week. Additionally, I attended regular weekend residential training and an annual residential week in the summer. At the same time, I was attending my local church where I was part of the serving team and encouraged to preach and function as a deacon. This kept me very grounded in the reality of parish life and offered me practical experience as well. I would happily recommend the ERMC to others, it was a broad experience.

However, I do think we need to look again at training. I feel strongly that it is neither viable nor fair, to put people into full time training if there are no full-time jobs for them at the end of it. The rivalry (and snobbery) between courses and colleges is ridiculous. We need to re-examine what is offered in the light of the future plans of our Church. If we are only appointing part-time priests, then we should only be offering part-time training. Full time training is wrong and puts people in a difficult position if they have nowhere to go at the end of their efforts. This is especially true if families are involved.

I enjoyed my curacy very much and was lucky to be placed in a rural parish in South Norfolk with a very warm church community. My training incumbent (TI) was brilliant, extremely supportive, and generous in training me and allowing me to lead worship. The community were very understanding and forgiving, as was he! This was not the experience of all my colleagues. I do not believe the matches made between TIs and curates were always made for the right reasons. My TI was also experienced in training which is effective. At the end of my curacy my TI took a sabbatical so that I was on my own for a period of time which was particularly good for me, and it is probably something all curates should experience before their first appointment.

There were two main challenges in my curacy, the first was housing. My family were asked to live in an inappropriate house by the diocese. A bungalow had been hastily bought for us, and it had serious problems with condensation which should have been apparent had a full survey been done on purchase. This resulted in black mould growing in many rooms. It caused a great deal of damage to clothing and furniture. My training incumbent responded to this very quickly, he could not have done more, and the archdeacon supported a move out of the house. Unfortunately, this meant that I had to live outside the parish which was sub-optimal but better than the mould.

Housing is so important and often overlooked. I have seen, repeatedly, curates being treated as an 'after thought' and there is no minimum standard of housing for them. Fortunately, my family were understanding, but I have seen it cause serious problems for others. Secondly, Covid, and nothing could be done, but it does make for a unique experience which is not always understood.

I have now moved to a different diocese, and I am the interim rector of eight parishes. I also have a day a week in a neighbouring benefice of another five churches as it is in vacancy. To some extent the experience is similar to my curacy, in so far of the environment and nature of my community, but I do not feel the same level of support, not least as I have fewer colleagues around. I am one of only two full-time priests in the deanery. The rest are either part-time or part-time non-stipendiary ministers (NSM), and so chapter meetings are limited, even the rural dean is part-time.

I am unfazed by the 'interim' nature of the position as I have things I could fall back on, if necessary, but not everyone does, and my parishioners are not happy to have it hanging over them. Others might be deterred from applying for posts which are so uncertain, but it is becoming the norm in rural areas.

My Tasks

Getting to know the local priest is a way for people to connect with the Church and with each other, but things have changed. People constantly talk about the days when the parish priest went from door to door or cycled around the village, but that is no longer possible, for two reasons. First, my parish covers just over 100 square miles, 150 if I add on the next benefice and secondly, the way we live has changed. Villages are often empty all day as people work elsewhere, when once they would have worked the land and been around and about the village. Now, even when they are at home, they are inside and not visible in the same way they once were. Meeting people means going to events which I do, but I cannot be at eight village shows at the same time, short of a miracle.

The mix of people living in rural areas is changing too, they are generally older and more affluent than in the past. Some villages have resident families but not all, at least one of my villages has no resident children although it does have a school. My work with schools is important but it is not visible to those in the Church in the same way as a Sunday school would be, or how it would be if they had children in the school themselves. Some of my villages are part of large estates who let the houses only on short term leases. This means that the population is often transient and makes finding parish officers quite difficult.

There is a decline in numbers since Covid, but also people will not travel to a neighbouring village. They may be happy to attend worship in their own church to which they are loyal, but they often refuse to go to the next one. As a result, the number of people in church each Sunday is fairly constant, but it does not reflect the fact that these are different people each week. My regular 'monthly' congregation is much bigger than the 'weekly' number suggests.

I offer a choice every Sunday of a Book of Common Prayer (BCP) or Common Worship (CW) communion somewhere in the parish. A few new people have started coming to our BCP service rather than travelling to a service in a neighbouring town. This is good for us, but it is not necessarily new believers, and of course, another church has lost out.

Finance is an ongoing issue. We do reasonably well but although we hit the target set for us by the diocese, we never hit the amount required for a full-time priest. The congregation were told before I arrived that they had to return to pre-Covid levels of giving in order to keep their priest, so we are constantly fundraising. I think once I leave, whether at the end of my contract or later, I will not be replaced with another parish priest. The diocese is talking about creating bigger 'ministry units' and as they have been unable to fill neighbouring benefices with House for Duty (HfD) priests, I think there may be a move to consolidate things further. It may not be our parish that drives the change, but it may be brought on them by neighbouring parishes failing to attract an HfD priest. On Sunday we dedicated a new board for our list of rectors as we had run out of space on the old one. I wonder whether mine may be the only name ever to be inscribed on the new furnishing.

Our churches are old and in need of attention – we have to pay for our own quinquennial survey which in itself can be a challenge before we even consider the action to be taken as a result. We have just managed to fix the heating in one church which was almost unusable in the winter as we have no church rooms to use as an alternative. If we could get support from central funds to maintain the buildings, which we are constantly told are a national treasure, a huge burden would be lifted, and we might just be able to afford more priests.

I visit people when I can, and this includes non-church goers. This is especially important, particularly for those no longer able to attend church. I visit the elderly and sick and will go to anoint and say prayers with the dying. I rely on people in the villages telling me what is happening though. You cannot know everything going on in over eight villages with multiple isolated farms.

I conduct a considerable number of weddings every year (eighteen in 2024) which are largely driven by picturesque churches and adjacent wedding venues. These do bring younger people in as they make qualifying connections, which I feel is good for the general worshipping community. It keeps us young and also gives the Church a more youthful appearance. We also do a respectable number of baptisms and funerals.

People still want to be buried in the churchyards which means a church funeral. I do fewer cremations, but the crematoria are a distance from the parish and traditionally people want to be buried in the village. Confirmations are not big in our area, and that is one of the more significant signs of drift. People baptise their children because it is a rite of passage, but confirmation is not seen in the same way outside the public school system.

Getting to know people locally and them meeting me, is a huge factor in occasional offices and where the parish really matters. People are happy to talk to me about their funeral arrangements knowing that it is likely to be me the local priest who leads the service. One lady told me she had been worrying about who would lead her funeral, but she is now happier knowing it will probably be a person she now knows. They know who they are getting and feel comfortable to make the necessary arrangements. I recently made such arrangements for a lady of 100 who still happily walks down to the shop for her paper every day, but whose family wanted to meet me and speak to me now, so they know me when the time comes. This is the same for weddings and baptisms.

I accepted the role with eight churches, but I also have one day a week in a neighbouring benefice which is in vacancy. Realistically, one day is not enough to do anything. As regards diocesan and Church leadership overall to be honest, I have mixed feelings. Some diocesan staff are really helpful and supportive, but in terms of the hierarchy perhaps less so. I rang safeguarding with a problem and was immediately directed to someone to help with the particular issue. But when there was a problem with the house (water coming through the ceiling) I had to chase facilities over three days to get any help. Newspapers stories about how the Church is spending its money, lands badly in the parishes where a few people are working hard to keep their church intact and their priest in post. I am still hearing about their feelings over Queen Anne's bounty! People also think I can influence the decisions of the Church commissioners. There is constant criticism of the archbishops and senior leadership, perhaps because people only hear sound bites on the news, some of which are not flattering. It is not helpful. This is the same for the appointment of senior people and central posts, even though this diocese has very few people centrally. It does not help when jobs advertised in news bulletins emailed out to parishioners, are for almost exclusively highly paid central secular posts whereas the priest posts, if there are any, are for part-time HfD or interim. I have to ask myself what message that is sending. Parishioners often resent the idea of money going to the diocese, not realising that it is this which is paying for their priests. Some would rather hold their money tight, than pay the diocese even though it means their clergy post will not be filled. They have grown to distrust them. They seem uncertain on what a bishop or archdeacon adds to the mix. Although bishops and the hierarchy may feel they have a crucial role and influence, the reality is, that on the ground, they have little relevance to the people in church.

They like it when they visit us, but I suspect they do not see what they are 'for' beyond ceremony.

Fewer bigger diocese would be better, with more consistency between them. They could share resources like finance, facilities and HR under fewer leaders which would save money which could go towards priests. Having so many diocesan bishops is ridiculous. It would also help share resources between richer and poorer areas. Well-attended churches in some of our poorer areas are making huge losses because the parishioners have nothing to give but their time and energy. Diocesan strategy is not seen as relevant locally, and even though I have just completed an entire sermon series on our strategy, I suspect most of my congregations would still look at you blankly if you asked about it, though may be that is just my preaching.

What is agreed in synod (general and diocesan) can feel very distant, and people may feel it has little to do with them, mainly because they have no say or any control over what happens. In my limited experience, PCCs do not appreciate their place in the structure or how they can make their voices count. Parishioners feel they have little influence over anything, and a number have asked me if I would mind if they joined Save the Parish movement so they can be heard.

The Fundamental Issues Which I Face

There is just not enough time to do everything that everyone wants me to do or that I would love to do. I have three schools, six in my extended area and it takes me nearly an hour to drive to the furthest one. I am a governor in one school and others would like me to be a governor too, but one is enough in terms of time consumption. Hospital visits take a half a day because they are all at a distance.

Generally, I think, there is little understanding of the realities of rural ministry among the Church leaders. Our training programmes and 'growth' initiatives seem to focus largely on urban or suburban settings. Often even 'rural' examples are in market towns. There appears to be little thought given to how to attract people to a village church, let alone one a mile outside the village, reached by an unmade, unlit road and which has no heating, water or loo. Turning it into a Post Office or café or yoga centre is also not the answer, it is a church first and last. Examples of successes highlighted are often urban, but it should be noted that evangelical churches are not what older people in rural areas want. My biggest area of growth is BCP. There is a decline in Church attendance. Sundays are not what they used to be as people have other things to do than go to church. Only counting Sunday attendance in the statistics each year is wrong. It fails to give a full picture. I speak to ninety plus children every week in collective worship, but that is not reflected in how we view interactions and does not show on statistical evaluations. People will often come to 'special' services when we might struggle to get them to come on a Sunday morning, but the success of these is barely recognised. If we counted 'points of contact' rather than 'bums on seats' on Sundays, it would be a different story.

There is complete disillusionment in this area as to why the Church cannot simply provide more priests especially as the money appears to be there when needed for other things in the wider Church. Priests in post are effective because the parish is about so much more than what happens on a Sunday. Speaking to parishioners in a vacant benefice about what they wanted a priest to do, the answer was 'vicary things' by which they meant just being a presence and being seen. Without a priest in post, those 'vicary things' cannot happen, so congregations fall away. In many ways Sunday mornings are the least of our work.

Our in-fighting over Living in Love and Faith (LLF) and even now, over women priests and other all other too familiar issues, covers us with shame and make us look hypocritical, especially to those of the younger generations which for them is probably our worst crime. They cannot believe that the Church discriminates against women and LGBTQia+ people in the way it does. It often is not the theological positions; it is how we are seen to behave towards others and each other, 'love thy neighbour as thyself'.

Editorial Comment: This contributor has raised many interesting issues and areas of importance. The importance of the TI is an area which should be noted, as also the ramifications of the Covid issue (which some feel that the Church guidance in this era was weak), and that many churches are national treasures and local and national government have some sort of helping responsibility in this area of concern and not place the burden on a few worshippers. It is also noted that the Church authorities are keen on attendance statistics, but the contributor rightly points out they only tell part of the story, and in the words of the contributor 'points of contact rather than bums on seats on Sundays, would be a different story'. A parish priest's work and service extend well beyond Sunday, which is a reminder that the Church is not a business venture. The writer mentioned 'vicary things' which means the priest is a presence within the community. It is also curious to recall that like other contributors this one points out that the rural Church is used more for baptisms, weddings and funerals than in towns, but laced with the criticism that despite the demands for money, fewer parish priests are provided, but there are always calls for well-paid places in diocesan house. It was also noteworthy that she refers to her 'contract' and the time she has there, the sense of an employee comes to mind, and her description about the sheer geographical expanse she covers is simply 'mind-boggling'.

Anonymous

Thank you for your request to me to express my views regarding the parish system. Most of my life has been in the parish, but I am having a two-year break before returning. We are old friends, and you know I have clashed on some parish matters with the archdeacon and bishop, and I would rather remain anonymous although they may quickly speculate that it is me writing this if it is ever read by them, so some of my details are going to be deliberately vague. I was ordained in the mid-1980s, I already had a first degree in theology, and I went to one of the more old-fashioned theological colleges for two years. I thought the training was good, not least when we had parish clergy come and speak to us, then we were fielded out to get a taste of parish life in different types of areas. My curacy was in a town, and I was lucky to have a vicar who was kind, generous, and never slow to point out both my strengths and weaknesses. He taught me to think carefully before I opened my mouth, and to use my youthful age to attract teenagers by opening a youth club. That sounds somewhat old fashioned today, but it worked, and many of those youth club members joined the choir, served at the altar, and since then one has been ordained, and many are still active in that church.

My first incumbency was in a similar town in the same diocese but 40 odd miles away. I am, as you well know, Anglo-Catholic and was thrilled to be attached to a church of this tradition. The town was slightly larger and there were two other parishes, another Anglo-Catholic church and an evangelical one, forming a small deanery with seven other rural parishes all of which are best described as middle of the road. These different styles of worship when I was first appointed were of little significance, and at area deanery meetings we would often tease one another about our varying styles of worship and always marked by good humour and friendship. They used to be meetings which I thoroughly enjoyed for the mixed companionship. We all agreed that visiting parishioners, the sick, new attenders, those who showed the slightest interest in church, newcomers into the area stood alongside the worship of God as our first duties.

It was about 10-15 years ago I became personally aware that there was a growing shortage of clergy, interregnums became widespread and longer, and parishes became linked into benefices. It first touched the rural side of the area deanery, as instead of seven members from what we townies called the 'country lanes' there were only two, giving the feeling our deanery was disappearing. Then it happened in town, following the resignation through old age of my fellow Anglo-Catholic priest, and the sudden sad death of our evangelical friend a short time after, the diocese decided for financial reasons one priest for both churches. He came from nowhere and unlike his low-church predecessor was a staunchly dedicated evangelical. He not only banned incense on his first day in the Anglo-Catholic Church, then rid himself of the sanctuary bells, and he only ever wore his surplus with hood and preaching scarf, and in that very Church derided the way they had worshipped. Behind the high altar he set up a film-screen so hymns could be displayed and his sermon notes (lasting over thirty-forty minutes), and the service shown because he had his own pattern of worship. Many in the congregation complained, but the archdeacon told them it was the new way. A few dared to approach the bishop and they had a similar but less bossy refusal for any action. My own congregation swelled overnight as the other congregation filled our pews, and the new evangelical minister, (he refused to be called a priest), complained to the archdeacon that I was poaching his church members. When he came to visit me on this matter, he was crystal clear that he was the gamekeeper catching the poacher in the act. I membered my first vicar's advice and stopped to think before I answered, but to no avail. A few months passed and then the bishop offered me what he called 'promotion', to move to a bungalow near diocesan house and become the spiritual guidance officer for clergy from these headquarters, on an enhanced salary, he did not use the word stipend. I gave this an hour's thought, then replied that I thought that was the bishop's task to guide his clergy in spiritual matters. He emailed a reply two days later telling me his 'job specification' had changed because he was drowning in many important management concerns, that he had seen it as 'advancement' for me, but the matter was dropped.

The deanery was enlarged with another rural based one attached, and the new evangelical minister was made rural dean without consultation, though none of the rest of us would have liked this post. He was constantly talking about the evangelical way of being the motorway to God. I kept my views to myself and sat quietly on the edge, but one new chap spoke out, only, he later told me to receive a letter from the archdeacon reminding him he was a priest-in-charge, not an incumbent. This was for me a 'management threat' the like of which I did not believe possible.

I wanted to leave the diocese, but I felt bound by my faithful long-suffering congregation. I was equally fed up with the financial demands which were fortunately taken care of by my lay members who had some financial acumen. One member of my congregation had been ordained, had finished his curacy and approached me as to whether I needed a curate or helper. I grabbed the opportunity and persuaded the new and less rigid archdeacon to accept my resignation and take him on as the rector, and after a brief interview this went through.

As you know, I was disliked by the hierarchy, but I am glad I never married or had any ambition apart from serving Our Lord, because I have just moved into the mission field in a dangerous and poverty struck area where I can work on at my duties without management control, and my only obedience is to serve my nomadic flock.

I appreciate you staying in touch, and hope this is not too much of a groaning 'has-been', but you asked my honest opinion about parish life which I shall be returning to in less than two years, but hopefully to another diocese, either to Winchester where we first met, or come to you in Norwich!

Editorial Comment: This contribution came as something of a surprise, from a priest this editor personally knew as a much loved and successful parish priest, he is in this section because his work in the mission field at the time of writing is just a few months to go, and he is returning after what he described as 'a necessary sabbatical' to recharge his batteries, though working in the area where he currently is, hardly credits the term sabbatical, as it is dangerous.

His main criticism of the work to which he has devoted his life, tends to focus on the new style of management coming to light in the Church's hierarchy, and the apparent upsurge of a demanding if not dictatorial form of Evangelism which is very pronounced in America. It is of course the archdeacon's role to sort out problems but to do it with prayer, sympathy and love, and this rang bells with another contribution of a retired priest who recalled a clash with a difficult archdeacon. This contributor recalled the bishop admitting his management work was immense, seemingly neglecting the critical pastoral role they play for frontline clergy. Naturally the Church needs management but not in the business sense, more in terms of the spiritual organisation, and parish clergy cannot perform their tasks well if they are treated as puppets on a string working for a demanding business firm. The second point he raises, relates to the possible damage done to the old hope that the Church of England is a wide umbrella, and in its comforting shade is the old fashioned high and low churches and those in between. No one group should be allowed to dominate and dictate to another, as we chose our routes toward God which can take different paths but without blocking others. It is tempting to say more prayer is needed and less forms to fill.

Humpty

Thanks for your letter and form which were passed to me when three colleagues I know have avoided answering. I decided to 'have a go', but I must remain anonymous, and I am happy to be known as Humpty my nickname which is only known by my closest friends.

I am now in my second incumbency where I have been for the last twelve years, I trained in Oxford, started life as a reader at a provincial university where I gained my doctorate in science, and where I felt a calling to be ordained. So, it was back to Oxford for a theological degree and a training to be a priest. I confess that I wondered why I felt called, and I know this as my perpetual shadow of doubt, but having worked in this parish this shadow is now a flickering reminder of past errors of judgment, and I feel called to serve Our Saviour on the streets and by-ways of wherever I am needed.

It is because I felt called to the priesthood that I have stayed a bachelor, simply because I decided that once I was ordained, I would have no substantial income to support a family and give them the necessary time. Now in my late forties I may have made a mistake, not in being ordained, but by not seeking a wife. The vicar in my next-door parish married in his curacy, and his wife not only supports his work, but she is the life and soul of the parish and loved by everyone.

Enough of my personal woes, you asked for some background notes, and I shall stop here. Your letter seeking contributions, has enabled me, or given me the excuse to raise the issue that parish priests are a vocation, called by God, not to earn large salaries, but just to have a roof over our heads and enough food to survive. This viewpoint led one of my friends to say 'Humpty, you would be more at home in a monastery', and I have been tempted to do just that, but a parish priest is here to serve the people in his area whether they attend church or not.

As a priest, as far as I am concerned, I am answerable to God, and God only. In my curacy my rector was fast approaching retirement age, and when I asked where he would retire to, he said he would not. He told me the story of a 75-year-old priest who he knew many years ago, who was asked by the bishop to retire for his own good, and he wrote back to the bishop stating that 'when one of your predecessors some forty years ago inducted me here he made no mention that it was a temporary position, I shall go when it is clear God is calling me home'. As such, I belong to what the archdeacon calls the 'old school' as I am happy to talk to the bishop for spiritual guidance and discuss parish affairs with the archdeacon, but I refuse to see them as my employers. The way I see my vocation was a calling by God to serve in the area to which I was called.

For reasons which confuse me, I am not exactly popular with the upper echelons of the diocese. On looking back, I had not helped my reputation when, as a younger man I was attending a diocesan synod and stipends were discussed. I argued that priesthood was a vocation, and all priests, be they curates, archdeacons, bishops, cathedral clergy should receive the same amount, only the expense accounts should differ. I even suggested that if anyone should receive more it should be those clergy raising young children. When an angry lay member said it would take away incentive for promotion, I told him being a deacon or priest or bishop was not a career but a calling. A quick show of hands clearly indicated I had a mere 10 per cent support, but was pleased, if not somewhat surprised, when one suffragan bishop offered support by agreeing with my sentiments.

I have tried to avoid cantankerous confrontations since, but I am often distressed at the recent development of our diocesan house always advertising posts with massive salaries, when at the parish level these days we are struggling to find clergy and the parish quota remains a constant headache.

Why I bothered to respond to your letter which reached me by a priest elsewhere in the diocese, was because I have serious issues coping with the growing control, I and others feel about the way we are virtually ordered how to conduct our ministry. In my current industrial and flat-filled parish, I have two churches as the second had been built as a daughter church in the 1930s in the suburbs, being a 13,000 plus populated parish. In my main church I take morning office at 8.30 am, and twice a week a 9.15 am said mass. In the daughter church I take evening office at 5.30 pm and hold one mass at 9.15 am each Sunday. During the weekdays the attendance is small, but I have never been alone, and in both churches, there are generally five to nine attending the offices and more at the daily masses. Both churches have sung mass on Sundays and are well attended, with evensong in the daughter church at 3.30 pm and in the main church at 6.30 pm, at least it only demands two sermons!

When it was proposed I should add another parish I refused on the grounds that I could not cope with more services and more visiting which I do on a daily basis. My first refusal was accepted but it has risen again, and this time the archdeacon explained I had little choice, that it had to happen for financial reasons. I argued that a post recently advertised for a 'strategy officer' by the diocese could pay for at least two more parish clergy, it was rebuffed by telling me that the old vicarage in the proposed new parish had already been sold.

I have become attached to the people of my parish, and I do not want to water-down my efforts and commitment to them. I have had to listen to the archdeacon at least eight times, and even the bishop, who is generally very gracious, but appeared suddenly bossy. I have the distinct feeling I am being seen as a nuisance, fighting against progress, and feel something of a pariah.

I know some of my clerical friends see me as a difficult person with my refusals, but in my main church the congregation has doubled over the last ten years. I do not say this to boast, but I put it down to three reasons. First, we are what is called a high church with incense and sanctuary bells, and I feel in this day and age the sense of what I call the 'mystique or mystery of the mass' is needed by many. The second is I think the importance of funerals. I often feel at baptisms and marriages I am the local witch doctor called upon to carry out a rite of passage. They are happy occasions, and I enjoy them and make new friends, but seldom new worshippers. Funerals hit and shock families, and as a priest I feel it is my duty to visit the bereaved as a priority, staying in touch long after the funeral, whether the service was in the church or the crematorium. I keep in my study what I call my 'obit book' which is a list of all the bereaved, and I call or write to them on the anniversary of their loss. On 'All Souls' evening I invite them to the service where they are invited to take a candle from the sanctuary and place it on our votive candle-stand with a prayer. This service is always packed and growing, and we had to purchase another votive-candle stand, and one of my church wardens, who is obsessed with numbers, reckons that the congregational growth comes from bereaved family members who attend more regularly. The third reason is the importance of visiting. I have a team of people who help here, and when a house is sold and new occupants move in, I am alerted and always knock on the door with a welcome, and I leave them with a paper regarding the church and the times of services. This would become impossible if my geographical responsibility is enlarged as even with this parish, I find time difficult, and it only works because I have three retired clergy who still work their socks off with some dedicated congregational members.

I know that I am seen by the diocese as a 'difficulty', and I may come over to you as a groaner and even a show-off, but I believe that if we abandon the old parish system or water it down by enlarging it, we are not only neglecting our duties but God's call to be his servants for the cure of souls.

Editorial Comment: This welcome but unanticipated contribution came as something of a surprise, but we have used his nickname of Humpty, and we have no idea of who he is but have respected his wish for anonymity. Though if this is ever read by his bishop or archdeacon it would not take much guesswork on their part, and Humpty is aware of this possibility. What made this contribution so useful was that in the current year of 2025 we have a parish priest who reflects the work of inner-city priests decades ago. He focused on the nature of vocation, a calling by God, and refuses to be ordered about by anyone except by his Christian conscience and his strong sense of calling. He sees the bishop as a person who offers spiritual advice and support, not as an employer with himself as the employed. As a young man he protested at the differences in stipend and received no support, but perhaps the time has come to study this issue with more care. An old, retired friend of this editor told him that his last five years of ministry was as the pastoral man in the cathedral deanery, and that he was paid much more, lived in a grand house, and did less work! More importantly, Humpty is a sharp reminder of a vocation and being called by God. He also passed on his letter from the project team to another who is the next-door parish, and which arrived the next day.

Humpty's Neighbour

My next-door parish is cared for by Humpty and for his sake I shall remain anonymous, but also because I have only been the priest-in-charge for less than two years, after having just served a one-year curacy I remain something of a novice in parish life. I have been told it is a two-year sort of contract or agreement to see how I cope. My appointment was a relief for Humpty, I am told by the archdeacon, because they wanted him to take it on as an extra parish. He also told me that Humpty, (not that he called him by that name which is a great secret) was old fashioned, and he would probably not be too pleased with a female priest. The archdeacon was wrong, because Humpty called on me as soon as I arrived, welcomed me, and said he was grateful to have such a pleasant neighbour and offered his help if I ever needed assistance. The diocese had sold the vicarage which is now owned by some well-off family who have a large notice on the gate announcing, 'The Old Vicarage', which struck me as a sad reflection on today's world. I live on the middle floor of a small block of flats.

I knew it was an Anglo-Catholic Church, but it proved more so than I had hitherto experienced. Humpty helped me out, and I attended one of his services. This led me to a small moment of depression, because his congregation was well over 100 whereas I was pleased if I had twenty or more. I went back to my vestry and found the registers to take home and study. I was simply stunned by what I read. Ten years before the average congregation had been around seventy to eighty, and the mid-week said communion was always a consistent seven to ten. The long interregnum and Covid period had seemed to have destroyed the normal attendance, and those who came were all over seventy as far as I could tell. It does not help me by blaming the Church authorities for this pain.

Having studied the registers, I was at Humpty's door the next day and he not only cheered me up but offered me advice. So, I talked and visited those who came to church, and that way I tracked down those who used to come and those who did not. It was not a great success, but it added a few more to Sunday worship. His next piece of advice proved invaluable. My parish had a large hall, and Humpty told me of someone who could run a youth club there, and my only job was to mix with those who came. Less than a year later I had a girls' choir, a small group of boys who acted as servers and cross bearers, and invented ceremonial jobs for others. Using this hall facility I re-started the local Mothers' Union (MU), let it out one evening to the chess club, a Judo and a dance club. All these efforts made the Church feel more part of the community and raised money.

I know the archdeacon was pleased, especially since we are closer to the financial targets than he forecast, and after my first year I anticipate being here longer than two years. Humpty and I have lunch together on Mondays, my place one week, his the second, and the third week at a local café. He has also introduced me to a retired priest who technically lives in Humpty's parish but willing to help me. This old priest is nearly 80 years old, but remarkably active and a man of long experience. His sermons go down well because he is always challenging, humorous and self-deprecating, he sometimes joins us for our weekly lunch which he dubbed the minor deanery.

I know that Humpty is not that popular with the archdeacon, and he has some critics amongst fellow clergy, but he is popular amongst the lay people, in and out of church. I have tried to mould myself on him, being out and about, knocking on doors, talking to people in the streets. I do not have a car since I hate the idea of driving through a busy city, and finding places to park is a nightmare. So, I often cycle which is a useful way for learning about my area, and if I see a person I know, I just pull over for a chat. I attend many meetings and always make sure that I am wearing a dog collar with darker clothes, so it does not look like a party dress.

My main concern is the future, I am hoping the bishop will let me stay on, but I have only met him once and all my directions centre on the archdeacon whom I see at least once every two to three months. The parish share has gone up again this year, and I am concerned that every time we are going to reach the target up it goes again. I found with the aid of my retired priest the help of a professional treasurer, but she never came to church which concerned me for a time, but recently she and her husband have started to appear on Sunday mornings.

There is little more I can say, but I must add I have found a splendid way of life I enjoy, and I pray to God this continues, that first I can stay here, and secondly, we do not collapse because of financial problems.

Editorial Comment: It was both amusing and a joy to read this follow up on Humpty, who evidently extended his ministry of love and care by acting as a mentor for this newcomer. It was interesting to note that it is a way of life she loves, and she indicates no displeasure that she lives in a flat, certainly living amongst her flock as part of her community. The points which spring to mind from her letter are her forebodings about her personal future and the financial problems of the parish. These are two issues the Church hierarchy always need to bear in mind with those who serve the Church and the will of God in the frontline of the Christian faith.

Unexpected Letter From Parish Priest's Wife

Editor's Note: This unexpected letter arrived with the widow asking for anonymity if we used her letter. This would have proved impossible as personal names and parishes were mentioned, so the letter was redrafted to keep anonymity, returned to the sender who replied she was happy with the contents. Throughout her text she refers to her husband by name, naturally, so she agreed that **** was acceptable.

Dear Andrew, I last saw you in the last century! As you know my lovely husband **** died two years ago so you may wonder why I am writing. I now live in a neighbouring parish, not moving too far because we made so many lifelong friends in the old parish. The parish priest showed me a letter asking for views on parish life, he told me he would not dare reply, and he put it in my paper basket by my desk.

A few days ago, when clearing out the basket I reread it, and as your email address was on it, and I thought I might add a few of my husband's thoughts and mine as well, because I saw myself as active alongside him in nearly thirty years of parish life. I guess you may not want this offering, and that would cause me no offence.

My husband **** loved his work as I did in helping him. Two parishes we served in and not a bad taste in our mouths at any time. We made so many friends I had over a hundred Christmas cards, and only five from family. The friendships were genuine, and I am still being invited to their homes for parties and dinners. The conversations always include memories of **** and the way he was so friendly, accommodating, and had baptised, married and buried so many loved ones.

As you know **** was no high or low churchman, somewhere in the middle, but he had good friends at the two extremes, and by using his well-known sense of humour often stopped growing rifts between them. He simply loved the work and was totally dedicated to preaching Christ, and his favourite biblical passage for all his life was I Corinthians 13 because it was based on love.

I know **** was becoming increasingly worried about the way that many parishes suffered long interregnums and many were joined together, and he upset the bishop who had explained that it was lack of ordinands. **** responded at this in a diocesan synod claiming that it all amounted to lack of money closing many of the traditional theological colleges, and during his ministry he had managed to convince five people to be ordained so the calling to priesthood was still alive, and because of money the church was not responding, so, he asked, where was the money going. My dear **** later admitted to me that he was a bit on the rough side, because he admitted those people who had gone through what he called part-time training seemed to be fine. Later when he had to see the bishop on another matter, he told me he was treated like a naughty schoolboy, and he was told to keep on doing his job as a 'local' priest and not be overly concerned about overall Church problems. When **** asked the bishop what the point of synod was, the subject was suddenly changed. It was not long after this that the new archdeacon appeared at the front door who gave **** a lecture on how much better the new training was, but although **** accepted this he asked why the shortage. He never answered this but went onto safeguarding and his scheme to make sure it was understood, because according to him, **** did not have sufficient notices in the church porch. All this from an archdeacon who had spent less than eight years in a parish. He also suggested that **** should seek some time with the spiritual guidance 'officer' at diocesan house.

I knew something was wrong, I popped my head round the door and asked if they would like a coffee, and **** said 'no thanks darling, the archdeacon is just going', the first and only time he had ever made such a response. It was two days later the surgery packed him off to hospital because of the continuous pains in his lumber region which he had ignored for so long, from there it turned out to be serious cancer and palliative care was the only thing on offer. ****'s only sorrow was leaving me alone and the future of the parish. Amongst his last words to me were about his clash with the bishop and archdeacon for which he blamed himself, but he said, and I shall never forget, 'these days there is a growing distance between the ordinary parish priest and episcopal care, and the archdeacons feel more like business management'.

His old friend a retired priest took the service and his pal the Roman Catholic priest gave an address followed by a eulogy. The funeral cost nothing as the local firm loved ****, the bishop wrote a letter of sympathy, some money came in from a diocesan charity. The archdeacon did not attend the funeral although the Church was so packed we had to have speakers outside when we ran out of space. The archdeacon wrote about how much time I had left in the vicarage and sent details about ****'s pension. It did not concern me because of my rich background I have plenty of money. I think I have said enough and use this only if you want.

Editorial Comment: This was one of the saddest letters we ever received and uncertain whether to include it into the project. It painted a picture of a successful parish priest, recalling he produced five ordinands and was clearly popular and a central figure in that community, even the undertaker made no charges. What caught the eye was ****'s last word to his wife, that 'these days there is a growing distance between the ordinary parish priest and episcopal care, and the archdeacons feel more like business management'. This is a theme which has been mentioned in many places especially in some heated contributions which we have not used. There is a feeling that contact between **some** bishops and parish clergy are waning, and **some** archdeacons have developed more of a business approach. The word some is in bold print, because this is the case only in **some** places.

Anonymous Letter

Dear Andrew,

We do not know one another, but I know your friend Alec, whose nickname at your old college was Frosty. I know you talked on the phone about some plan with some others of bringing people together for their views on parish life. As you know, Alec is not well, and he passed your message onto me, a very young priest in charge of a small-town parish, with the idea of making a response, warning me to keep it confidential, assuring me that you would accept this plea. Alex retired here many years ago, kept the parish going during a lengthy interregnum, and now he sits at the back of the congregation, but over the last few months I have taken him communion after the Sunday morning service.

I do not want to follow all the suggestions about writing of past experience but would like to express a couple of my frustrations in this email-letter which you may or may not find useful, and no offence if you bin it. The first issue is personal to me. I was trained in a regional course just over two years. I had a personal tutor, went on various courses mainly at weekends, but one was a much lengthier residential effort which was enjoyable. I did various biblical studies, some Church history, doctrine, and spent some weekends attached to different types of parishes. My personal dilemma is a matter of self-doubt about my knowledge of the faith, which has made my writing of sermons difficult, and sometimes shuts me down in discussion groups when I should be saying more. A classic example was in one group the synoptic gospels were raised, and although I knew three of the four Gospels are known as the synoptic ones, I had no idea about the complexity of the study, and not even which one was written first. When I was asked about docetism, I had no idea what they were talking about. At the academic level I feel I have fallen short, but this personal dilemma is even wider, in so far that at first no one had explained the nature of the last rites to me, and I was at a loss when talking and praying with people in their last moments of life. My main stay has been to flee to Alec for help, but as you know he will not be with us much longer. I am trying to remedy these problems by reading some of Alec's old textbooks, but I still feel wobbly and uncertain about my abilities to cope with the better informed. I have even started to read a book on comparative religions because my parish has quite a few Muslims and Hindus. I have spoken to another person who trained with me and she, like me, feels a gap in sheer knowledge and information. I have been lucky on one score, Alec failed his degree at college, gained a diploma and was ordained two years later. He was always angry with himself for his academic failure, so he decided to do a London BD external degree through a correspondence organised by a place called Wolsey College now long shut. I gather that is how you met because you marked and corrected his New Testament Greek papers. He has left me all his course papers which I am finding useful, but my main problem remains because I lack confidence mainly because I received in my opinion insufficient training, even though I was commended when we finished. I think the Church should arrange longer and more in-depth training.

My second issue, which is why I also want to keep anonymous, is that when I raised this problem with the archdeacon, he told me my anxiety would pass as I was just a young woman learning as she worked. He also told me that dear old Alec belonged to the old school who were rapidly leaving us. At least when I raised this with the bishop, he gave me a copy of *Peake's Commentary* and sent me a list of books I might find helpful. With the archdeacon I was made to feel more like a struggling schoolgirl telling me to keep my chin up. My personal anxiety was coming close to depression which some parishioners noted, but not the archdeacon. Whenever he calls in, he never asks how my new studies are going, he wants to see how congregational numbers are doing and our finances. I know from clergy friends that not all archdeacons are like this, but this one is driving me mad. I suspect you may be tempted to think I am making this too personal, but as a young new priest I also need encouragement and support. When he looked at the registers, he noted the numbers had dropped drastically, and when I pointed out that this occurred during Covid he simply brushed it aside telling me of other churches had rapidly recovered. My congregation on a Sunday is small, only about twenty-five to thirty people, and no youngsters, and they are expected to raise thousands of pounds for the parish quota. In fact, please treat my letter lightly, because on reading it I feel fed up with myself for moaning, but I am not as happy as I used to be. It would be good to know your thoughts.

Editorial Comment: The first thing was to reply, offering some help suggesting some theological and biblical commentaries, and some heartfelt, encouragement and condolences which were sincere. This young priest has started a youth club, kicked off coffee mornings with a group of young mothers, and a club for the retired all in the past year since her first letter arrived many months ago.

She made two important points that the new form of training for ordination on some courses, especially the younger ones, probably needs to be deeper and longer. The love of God can be passed on by those who have no education at all, but when a priest is expected to stand in a pulpit and preach, lead meetings, and answer questions because they have been made Church leaders, they will feel safer and more able if they have been well prepared.

It was interesting to note that her archdeacon did not reflect all archdeacons as some are rightfully more pastorally minded and caring, but there was a warning here, reflected elsewhere in some replies, that they must avoid been seen as business managers.

Anonymous Rural Rector

I am the rector of a rural benefice of churches, a post I have held for the past ten years. Before this I was vicar of a single-church urban parish and served my curacy in a town setting with two church buildings. I have been ordained for seventeen years.

My experience of the Christian faith in my formative years was very limited. My family were not church goers although they happily referred to themselves as Christians. An early memory was following a freak accident at the age of 5, which required hospitalisation and my mother telling the nurse completing the admission form that I was 'Church of England'. As was the approach of the day, I was automatically a member unless I opted out, but the nearest I got to any form of worship was listening to my maternal grandfather whistling along to hymns as he watched *Songs of Praise* on the BBC.

I can remember very little of any formal religious education at school; vague recollections of hearing the better-known Bible stories in primary school and studying the subject to O-Level in high school. God certainly has a sense of humour, as it was the only O-Level I failed! I took the view at that time that maths, English and the sciences were more important.

My first meaningful experience of the Church in the parish was when my now wife and I bought our first house in a small Norfolk village. This was during the 1980s when house prices were booming, and we had to make a choice to either pay for a wedding or make a deposit on our first home. We chose the latter, but within a year approached the local vicar to discuss marriage. We had no idea where the vicarage was and knocked on the door of the large, old house adjacent to the Church (as you would!) only to discover that this was the old vicarage; we were redirected to the modern vicarage on the new housing estate. I look back on our first meeting with the parish priest as a seminal moment in my life, and every time I now sit with a young couple seeking marriage, I am reminded of that occasion some forty years ago. After taking my details, the vicar turned to my now wife and asked for hers; when she gave the same address as me his pen froze on the page, and he peered at us over his half-moon glasses saying nothing. We squirmed in our seats fully expecting a lecture on 'living in sin' but after a moment he laughed and told us that his own daughter was living with her boyfriend. At the end of that meeting he encouraged us to attend a Sunday service once or twice before our wedding day which we duly did. I often wonder whether I would have taken the path to a committed Christian and eventually to ordination if our first vicar had not gently encouraged us to experience the Church community in the parish. The Church and faith soon became central to our lives, and we engaged with all aspects of church life, and we felt very much part of a loving community. I was the crucifer and a server at the altar, a member of the PCC and eventually a church warden.

Ten years after this first encounter with faith, I began training as a reader, but I was soon aware that I was training for the wrong ministry. The day of my licensing was the last day I saw my father who attended the service in the cathedral and took communion for only the second time since leaving his boarding school. Almost the last words he said to me were 'there we are son; I can die in peace now as I have made my communion'. Little did we know that he would die from a sudden heart attack just two days later. It was a very difficult time for me, coping with my loss, supporting my distressed mother and family and trying to make sense of it in the light of my faith and my two-day old reader ministry. What did come out of that period was the very clear understanding of the centrality of the sacraments and an affirmation of the call to be a minister of them.

Within three years of my licensing as a reader, I began the process of discernment for ordination which I progressed through very quickly; indeed, before I went to the Bishops' Advisory Panel (BAP) my Diocesan Director of Ordinands (DDO) got a little nervous and looked to me to confirm that I felt ready. I enjoyed the experience of selection as I felt very much in God's hands and that His will would become clear to those entrusted to this ministry of discernment. I was recommended for training and began part-time study with the Eastern Region Ministry Course, part of the Cambridge Theological Federation.

Following ordination, I took up my title post in an Anglo-Catholic town parish. We had a ministry team which consisted of the rector, an associate priest and me as the assistant curate as well as a non-stipendiary minister and a reader. My experience of curacy was a very positive one and I had a particularly good relationship with my stipendiary colleagues. My training incumbent was very experienced and had worked with several curates previously and we quickly developed a close and friendly working relationship. Our associate colleague was a very wise soul who had been ordained for nearly forty years having trained at Kelham Theological College, and although he was very unwell and sadly died before the end of my curacy, he taught me a great deal about the priestly life and parish ministry. The first time I met him he told me that there was nothing I could do so wrong in my curacy that the rector could not put right. It gave me permission to trust in myself, trust in God and trust in my training incumbent; they were wise words which have stayed with me and which I have used in conversation with my own curates over the years. I truly valued the freedom I was given as a curate and the rector soon realised that I was not someone who needed to have my hand held all the time. I grew as a priest by being given the freedom to grow into the priest God had called me to be, not to be somehow formed into a clone by a training incumbent. I had that freedom, but I also had the assurance of the safety net he provided – if I were to fall, I would not fall far enough to cause lasting damage. The parish gave me a solid grounding in the centrality of the daily office, administration of the sacraments and importance of the pastoral ministry. We celebrated communion three times on a Sunday and three times during the week and had many weddings, funerals and baptisms for which we had an open-door policy; my training rooted me an understanding of my priesthood as an expression of God's love to the community in which I served, making God present through my presence in people's lives. My training incumbent has remained a close friend, and we meet socially with our wives and take an annual retreat together which is always a special time.

At the end of my curacy, I was appointed as the incumbent of a single-church urban parish. It had a modern church building built thirty years previously with the intention of bringing together two former congregations, one from the Anglo-Catholic tradition, the other from a 'low church' tradition. Many of the trappings from the Anglo-Catholic church had been retained with a statue of Mary in the lady chapel, a tabernacle for the reserved sacrament, a large reredos on the wall behind the main altar, a votive candle stand, and an extensive range of vestments. However, it soon became clear that the current congregation had little or no understanding of the liturgical significance of these items. The church was used by several community groups during the week who had their own key and came and went as they pleased. The congregation considered this to be a great outreach, but they had minimal interaction with the groups, and I came to feel more like a community centre caretaker than a parish priest. It was a 'gathered' congregation with the majority living outside the parish which from my perspective impeded any real engagement with the local community because they did not live there. I was frustrated that I was not able to be the pastoral parish priest I felt called to be and uncomfortable with what I considered to be a lack of the sense of the sacred in the building. My situation was not made any easier by a difficult relationship with one of the retired priests who lived in the parish, and a lack of any real support other than from my former training incumbent and another priest from a previous parish who is now one of my closest friends. One highlight from my time there was the opportunity to work with my first curate although I am certain her experience was impacted by some of the tensions I felt.

After four years I knew it was time to move on and I now look back on that period as a second curacy. I am very aware that I made mistakes in that time, and they were perhaps the mistakes that all priests make in their early years, but I had no senior colleague to fall back on. I suspect the shortening of curacies to one, three-year placement rather than two has probably caused emotional and spiritual harm to many clergy who were cast straight into their first incumbency with little support.

The move to my current benefice has been a revelation to me. At last, I truly feel I am in the place I am called to be with a small but active church community with committed congregations who love God, care for their church buildings as sacred places, engage with the wider parishes and work well together as a benefice.

My ministry is rooted in pastoral care with visiting and home communions a high priority. I dedicate a great deal of time to preparing wedding couples and I am always pleased when they comment on how much it is appreciated. I am concerned that in the past few years the number of weddings has fallen from around fifteen to twenty each year to five or less. Some of this is due to the competition from venues offering wedding packages, but financial pressures also have a part to play. There is also a belief amongst some couples that they cannot marry in church if they are not regular attenders, part of an increasing ignorance about the Church and what we offer and stand for. Church funerals have been on a downward trend ever since I was ordained; whereas twenty years ago the list of funerals at the local crematorium was largely dominated by religious services, now they are in a minority. The growing popularity of civil celebrant services and direct cremations is concerning, not only as a sign of declining faith but also the lack of pastoral care and support they offer. The falling number of baptisms is another indication of a growing separation between the Church and the communities it serves, and a generation maturing into adulthood who have received less meaningful religious education and contact with the Church than previous generations.

This is why the reduction in clergy through fewer vocations and cost-cutting measures in the dioceses is such a concern and the model of increasing the size of benefices and spreading clergy ever thinner is a disastrous one in my opinion. Oversight ministry may suit many clergy who avoid pastoral ministry and are happy in front of their computer screens all day, but in my experience, it is not providing people with what they truly value – a personal relationship with the parish priest and the trust which is thereby nurtured. I believe the Church flourishes when the priest 'knows and is known' in the community. This is not to undermine the growing involvement of the laity in ministry, but I do not believe it can successfully replace the role of the priest. As one of my church wardens said to me quite recently following a period of ill health on my part, 'as laity we can keep things going, organise service cover, manage the finances and the practical matters. What we cannot do is provide the pastoral ministry. That is what is missing when you are not here'.

In this post I have had the opportunity to work with my second curate which was a rewarding and joyful experience, but the change in the demands placed upon her compared to my first curate a few years earlier was marked. In my opinion there was too much writing, reflecting and journaling which inhibited the genuine learning that comes though 'doing' and 'being' as a natural exercise rather than seeing every visit to a parishioner as a pastoral encounter which must be pulled apart, analysed and written about. The central oversight by the diocesan training team felt very forced and unnatural and essentially a box ticking exercise. The danger in the very controlled training environment which now exists is that we produce clergy who are good at planning and managing structures and routines but who struggle to cope with the very messy, challenging, unpredictable nature of everyday ministry. I also question the process around placing curates in title posts – both of my curates came to me following a request from the bishop that I consider taking responsibility for their training. I did not register an interest with the DDO or prepare parish profiles to try to 'sell' the parish to prospective curates. I am aware that several curacies fail each year due to a breakdown in the relationship between curate and training incumbent which is devastating for both parties. A system whereby the bishop or archdeacon is trusted to decide the most appropriate training parish for a curate would seem much better than the competitive tendering which seems to have become the norm, and the training incumbent should be trusted to undertake that training without excessive interference from the centre.

I consider myself very fortunate to have served under several bishops and archdeacons all of whom were very competent, supportive and pastoral, but in parish ministry there is always a tension between what the church members in the parishes consider to be important and what the Church hierarchy often request or expect, and there is no doubt that the administrative burdens for both parish clergy and parishioners have increased significantly in recent years. With training expectations, safeguarding, DBS checks and GDPR regulations, the demands on individuals who are volunteers is immense. Consequently, we struggle to find people prepared to take on the roles of church warden, PCC treasurer and secretary. The financial burden is also becoming untenable. My parishes have a total population of around 3,000 people, and we are asked to contribute over £72,000 to diocesan funds in parish share and that is in addition to funding the maintenance and day-to-day running costs of our heritage buildings, admin costs and any local missional projects we might be keen to pursue. As a system it is unsustainable, and there needs to be a complete overhaul of the system of Church funding, with serious thought given to how the Church commissioners allocate their funds, which for some years now has been weighted towards mega-projects based on business models and analysis of projected returns, and risks turning us into the Church of England Plc. My personal view is that there needs to be a step change in the Church with a re-empowering of the parish system, much greater financial support from the Church commissioners and a return to a focus on the local. I am not aware of any example where a parish has lost its priest or been swallowed up into a larger benefice with fewer clergy and has grown in attendance or financial resilience. There seems to be a general acceptance that in parish ministry we are there to manage decline, taking on more parishes as the congregations reduce in each. The temptation is to see centralisation as the answer, but I suggest that it is part of the problem. The Church of England has always been a local church for it is there that relationships are made; communities are built and disciples nurtured. It can only be done face to face through loving pastoral, personal ministry by both clergy and laity.

As I look back on my Christian journey I do so with gratitude for people, not processes, and I fear the Church of England has become over reliant on process. I remember that first encounter with the priest who married my wife and I where we were welcomed not judged; I remember the Church community where we set up our first marital home who welcomed and nurtured us and taught us what the love of Christ means; I remember those who walked the path of discernment with me to first reader and then ordained ministry; I remember those I trained alongside, all of us from vastly different backgrounds, churchmanship and personal experience but united by a desire to be faithful to our calling; I remember the clergy in and beyond my training parish who showed me by example the privilege and the challenge of priestly ministry; I remember the curates I have walked alongside who have taught me as much as I have taught them.

Above all, I remember the parishioners I have sought to serve, those I have laughed with, those I have cried with, those I have shared the sacraments with, those I have baptised, those I have married, those I have sat with on their deathbed and those I have buried. A daily privilege and a challenge and a way of life I have never regretted. A way of life rooted in people not a process; a way of life threatened by the loss of the parish system.

Editorial Comment: This positive and full contribution offers many interesting insights which need little comment as he puts it so directly. Some of his observations could not help but catch the eye. When he refers to the 'open door policy' it has always been the understanding that the parish priest baptises, marries and buries anyone within their parish whether they attend church or not. It is often this service to the community which not only makes the parish central to community life but can bring in new members. There is, he noted 'a belief amongst some couples that they cannot marry in church if they are not regular attenders', that many funerals are taken by humanists, but he rightly notes that the 'Church flourishes when the priest knows and is known'.

He expressed some concern over the shortening of time spent as curates which has also been noted by many, with one wit saying 'we need more time to make our mistakes'. He notes that the older system of oversight by the bishops and archdeacons was probably better than the more 'management style' of diocesan teams. He is equally concerned about the financial ramification in the new age, pointing out that 3,000 local residents need to find £72,000 for the parish quota, but the task falls upon the fewer people who attend church which is not only 'mind-boggling' but a serious headache for the priest and the faithful. The administration of a parish with these burdens can distract from the parish priest's vocation of offering the love of God and care for the community.

Chapter Two

Views of Retired Parish Clergy

Introduction

One colleague once said that the retired clergy are always disgruntled about something because they are old, another that they felt guilty because their generation have created the mess that seems to be happening in the decline of numbers, loss of young ordinands, and the changes in the traditional parish system. One other in our discussion group said that in his neck of the woods many churches would be totally inactive without the help of retired clergy. It was agreed that the vast majority of retired clergy have given their lives to the priesthood and mainly in parish churches, and they have seen the best and the worst, watched the ups and downs, and their views should be respected. Retired senior bishops are often used in retirement to chair some national issues which need a balanced guide with experience. It made sense therefore to enlist the views of retired clergy, especially those who are still voluntarily active and those who regularly attend their local parish for worship. They bring with them a life-long's experience but are also well aware of how the current system of parish life is struggling. Some contributors in this chapter who were asked to outline their training and past experience offer by doing so, some outstanding insights which offer a contrast or comparison as to what is happening today. This offers many insights, including the changes in theological training, which often continued post-ordination, the value of curacies, and a developing of wide experience. As with many others there are fears and also hopes for the current situation.

The Revd. Jennifer Elliott de Riverol

My Background

The Revd. Jennifer Elliott de Riverol Cert Ed., Dip TEFL. M.A. Norwich diocese.
Spiritual Director and Voluntary Chaplain East Anglia's Children's Hospice.
Licensed Lay Minister: 2000–2011 San Martin de Porres, La Palma, diocese in Europe.

Deacon: All Saints Anglican Church, Tenerife with responsibility for San Martin de Porres, La Palma 2011–2012. Assistant curate: as above 2012–2015. Priest-in-charge: as above 2015–2017. Rector: Briningham Benefice, including Brinton, Hunworth, Stody, Swanton Novers, Thornage 2017–2020. From 2020 to the present day: permission to officiate in the diocese of Norwich and the diocese in Europe. Tradition: Anglo-Catholic but tolerant towards other traditions.

Ordination Training

I had been a licensed lay minister for eleven years when I began training for ordination. This was via the Eastern Region Ministery Course, based in the UK. I was required to attend residential weekends and summer courses over a period of two years, whilst remaining in full time employment as a high school teacher. Essays of 3,000 words had to be submitted on subjects such as the Old Testament, New Testament, ageing, ethics, life and service, the Christian God, further Christian doctrine, bereavement and preaching.

I was allocated a personal tutor, who would liaise with me and visit me (in La Palma) to hear me preach and observe me leading services. I also undertook placements in the UK, at St Christopher's Hospice London, and later St Stephen's Church, Norwich.

Curate Under Training

In the diocese in Europe, there are limited opportunities for hands on observation. In my case, my training incumbent lived in Tenerife, whilst I lived in La Palma, different islands. I was officially a curate at All Saints

Anglican Church Tenerife, whilst having responsibility for the Anglican congregation in La Palma. Apart from video links, my training incumbent would fly over from Tenerife once a month to lead a Eucharist service, and we would discuss my course work and other pastoral matters. I also attended meetings with him in Tenerife and we would meet at our archdeaconry synods which took place in mainland Spain over a four-day period. I would lead confirmation and Lent courses and help to organise social events centred around Easter, Christmas and so forth.
Additionally, and as a fluent Spanish speaker, I was encouraged by the local Roman Catholic community to participate in cultural and Church events. I participated especially in ecumenical matters in the week of prayer for Christian unity. This was linked with my role as chaplain at the local Spanish hospital. I was also invited to give talks in English and Spanish at Spanish high schools and at the RC seminary for ordinands in Malaga.

Observations On the Parish System

I returned to live permanently in the UK in 2017 to take up the part-time house for duty position of rector for the Briningham benefice, comprising: Briningham, Brinton, Stody, Hunworth, Thornage, Swanon Novers. My stipend was £312 per calendar month. I felt enthusiastic about being back in the UK and serving God through this ministry. I embraced the challenge. In my area was Brinton Hall, Stody Hall and Briningham Hall, where some of the church wardens lived, and they held some power in the local community, being wealthy and large landowners. I was stepping into new territory and often felt unsupported. I had come from a working-class background and had lived abroad for over forty years. I was often reminded that the bishop had said at my licensing and induction that I would not be alone in my role as rector.

As well as taking two services on Sundays I also led services at Swanton Care Home and Thornage Hall; the latter being a residential for people with special needs. I tried to keep Tuesdays and Wednesdays as my days off but inevitably, juggling six parishes and fitting in with others' duties, plus taking funerals and so on, I soon found myself working more than my part-time status had originally required me to do. All the parishes wanted their own PCC meetings, Harvest festivals, carol services and so on.

I had inherited a situation of five out of six parishes using BCP for their main Sunday service. I did not think this encouraged mission and outreach in the community, but I accepted this arrangement when I arrived, and I hoped that in time we might develop other service formats, for example for fifth Sundays when the benefice service took place.

An LLM was in place when I arrived and I was looking forward to working with her, but within a few months, some of the parishes had made formal complaints about her to the warden of readers and she was invited to resign. Apparently, she had been, allegedly, unreliable.

One of the church wardens an AWA led an informal service once a month, which coincided with a BCP one in the same village. This later collapsed but perhaps we might have been able to develop something similar in the future.

I had assumed that monthly benefice services would encourage parishioners to travel from their 'home' church to whichever church was holding a service; a distance of a couple of miles at most. Sadly, this was not the case. The majority of worshippers only worshipped at their local church, so benefice services were really only for those attending their 'own church'. Consequently, Church attendance was quite poor on the whole.

The financial aspect of each parish having to raise a large amount of money to cover the parish share, plus maintaining the Church fabric, added to a scenario of unhealthy competition among the parishes. I felt that there was a lack of showing generosity and love towards our neighbours, by not sharing resources.

In the deanery of Holt, I found myself with another female colleague when I arrived, but she retired soon after my arrival. Among my colleagues was someone who was not in favour of the ordination of women, and I found communication with him difficult. On the whole, I did not feel supported and nurtured by the rural dean, my colleagues and some parishioners. Such was the pressure I felt that I found myself having to take sick leave because of anxiety and depression. This was mainly because of some 'toxic' personalities in my parishes, some of whom were not Church goers but felt it their duty to take part in the life of the church.

The final straw was when a church warden and a group of non-church goers informed me that they no longer wished me as rector to lead the service which took place at the pill box on Remembrance Sunday. This was traditionally led by the incumbent. I questioned the authority of those who were making this decision, and I was told that it was in line with new measures being promoted by the British Royal Legion. I really do not think this was the case and concluded that the matter was really to do with 'power wielding'.

An official complaint about me was then made to the bishop, instigated not by the church warden but by 'the non-church goers'. Thus, the archdeacon was contacted, and he held a meeting (without me present) with the people who had been instigating the trouble. It was extraordinary that I was never made aware about the exact nature of their complaints and in the end, I felt that the only course of action to save me from further anxiety was to resign, which is what I did. The archdeacon would later tell me that he thought he had handled my case badly. I believe this was true because my side of events had not been taken into consideration. Had there been more transparency and communication, I would have been willing to continue in my role. I felt totally let down by the Church and the parishes. I was not consulted and not supported.

Finally, I would like to summarise my thinking. I had been told during my time as rector that some of my churches were being run like 'pony clubs', pony clubs being part of the social fabric. This may have been true! However, I sought to see the presence of God in everything around me and tried to share with others that it is really God who is in the driver's seat, not us.

I feel that the basic problems among my parishes were caused through the lack of spirituality, Bible study and prayer. Had I stayed, I would have tried to bring people together in this way. Additionally, being responsible for six parishes on a part-time basis in not tenable or desirable. It is barely possible on a full-time basis if one is really God's agent for 'the Cure of Souls'. It was simply too large for one individual, which is happening in many areas, and the Church authorities seem to ignore this critical factor. Parishes should be seeking the presence of God in the world and promoting the message of Christ and not be overly concerned about raising money or the views of non-church goers.

Editorial Comment: This contributor draws attention to the fact that it is not always easy being a parish priest, it is not just a matter of cream teas and sherry parties, but as in national matters it is the same at local level, where one can feel enmity and opposition, and not understand where and why. This female priest even ran up against hostility because of her gender, and some non-church attenders complained to the local church authority. It was poorly handled even by secular standards, when normally the ecclesiastical authority should be more transparent and even compassionate. It also appears that the complaints came from non-church goers. She noted the headache for her of having to be a fundraiser because of the financial demands imposed on parish life and made more complex and difficult by being responsible for six parishes. For her, like any priest, the vocation should not be about raising funds but more to do with 'spirituality Bible study and prayer' to use her own words. In short, a parish priest's main role is to bring God and his people together, not keep asking for cash.

Anonymous

This contribution came from a retired priest now aged over 80 years and who started his training in King's College London, and who has requested to keep his thoughts entirely anonymous. Throughout his adult life he held a variety of posts from curacies to incumbencies in town and rural areas, and until quite recently continued his work during retirement in his words by 'visiting, worship and pastoral care'.

Today, in the area in which I reside there are eight parishes, and they are ministered by two stipendiary clergy. In a nearby deanery there are currently two stipendiary clergy who are serving nineteen churches.

Curates these days anticipate being given their first living not of one parish, but several with their various churches, which is a common situation in these developing years.

Some of the parishes in my area are HfD, and they are often based on a contract of working only half the week. This has had natural consequences, so far that it means that the church building is rarely used for funerals, and a secular private cremation and burial ground has become popular in this area.

There has been a desire by the hierarchy not to favour the ministry of the retirees; yet we are experienced, cheap and available. One thought may be that the retirees are tired of the red tape and so do not apply for Permission to Officiate (PTO) and all the other forms which need to be filled in. This lack of clergy has led to the major difficulty of the inability to contact or find clergy, which has led to the consequence of handing services to lay people, humanists, and many others who are paid for their services, and more to the point has detracted from the parish church being regarded as critical and as an essential community support.

I believe that the present situation will and has already started the demise of the rural church. The emphasis on the deanery is pure nonsense as people will not travel to seek the Church elsewhere which happens to be holding a service on a particular Sunday. People have become over centuries accustomed to their own local church, and do not appreciate the cost, the uncertainty of attendance, not to mention the severe weather and driving around looking for the opened church that day. The demise of weekly Sunday worship to perhaps once a month with the vagaries of service times, means that some will travel to one parish church 6 miles away which maintains a service at the same time each week.

It is difficult to know whether the above issues are part of the policy of the Church of England, and I have little to no confidence in the bishops or the archdeacons. Considerable energy goes into safeguarding and sexual issues, both on their part and on the demands which they make on their clergy. I would refer to Father Julian Browning's sermon at All Saints Margaret Street on 6 October 2024, where he was critical of the LLF project as it led to disagreement rather than any sense of concord.

It should be of no surprise that my experience as a retiree with PTO during a lengthy interregnum has resulted in a diminished ministry. I felt that I was in limbo, but I am now able to continue with active PTO, with some hoping I will continue to visit them, but I am 'Learning to let go and let God'. I cannot but help suggest reading *The Contemplative Minister* by Ian Cowley (2015), a book meant for clergy warning that there are currently very few posts in full-time ministry which do not require a heroic combination of stamina, multitasking, and changing management. The book demonstrates how to grow into a contemplative minister prioritising a relationship of deepening love with God, a major point which must not be lost in these changing times.

Editorial Comment: In this person's experience there is a sense of anguish and sadness at the disappearance of the traditional parish ministry, not least as the centre of life has moved from the community to the larger area of the deanery, which in rural cases can have a vast geography. This is a common theme for many who observe with interest what is happening within the Church of England. He draws attention to the house for duty and working only 'x' number of days, clearly indicating that the Church authorities over whom he pulls no punches, no longer see a parish priest as a vital fulltime post, but part-timers obliged to enlist anyone who might help. Many will agree with his views on the growth of red tape and some surprised that he feels the mission of retired clergy is not appreciated by those in 'higher places', the latter which may be, hopefully, more of a local issue. Finally, he draws our attention to the vulnerability of rural or more remote areas, where often the parish church has been the main cornerstone for developing a sense of community let alone as a critical place for worship.

The Venerable John Rawlings

Personal Details

The Venerable John Rawlings, Ordained Deacon 1970. Priest 1971, in Rochester Cathedral. Curate Rainham, Kent 1970–1973, Rochester diocese. Curate Tattenham Corner and Burgh Heath 1973–1976, Guildford diocese. Chaplain RN 1976–1992. Vicar Tavistock and Gulworthy 1992–2006, Exeter diocese. Rural dean of Tavistock deanery. Archdeacon of Totnes 2006–2014, Exeter diocese. Retired September 2014. PTO since. Married 1969 and son and daughter born while in first curacy. Churchmanship Anglo-Catholic upbringing and background, now I would describe myself as modern liberal Catholic.

Training

King's College London and St Augustine's College, Canterbury 1966–1970. The AKC (Associate of King's College) course was an excellent foundation/formation for those who aspired to be parish priests but who were not particularly academically gifted. It was a comprehensive introduction to every branch of theology, biblical study and its attendant subjects. Being a full-time course in the colleges and with a requirement to live in the theological hostel for at least the third year (I was there in my first year as well) meant being in an environment of living in a community, with communal prayer, meals and recreation. In my second year I lived in a house owned by a parish in North London with four other students on the course. Contact with the parish priest, who had been an AKC student in the 1930s, was a helpful insight into parish life in an environment very different from where I had grown up in Surrey. It also gave me an opportunity to meet his daughter who became my wife, now fifty-five years married. A great bonus to the training course itself.

Curacies

Being a curate in Rainham Kent, was a very good part of my life and allowed me to gain experience in the first three years of my ministry which has stood me in good stead for over fifty years. It was in a sense a traditional English parish. Unlike most places today it was a single church benefice with vicar, senior curate and junior curate. A small town/large village but growing all the time with new housing. Sundays 8.00 am holy communion, 10.30 am parish communion, 6.30 pm evensong, with a choir of a dozen or so most of the time. There were many weddings, funerals, and baptisms every year. Morning and evening prayer was daily in church, mostly with just the three of us. The vicar was keen that we never lost the Greek we had studied at King's College London, so on weekdays if there were no lay people for evening prayer, we read the second lesson in Greek. There was great encouragement to visit people in their homes. Visiting was seen as an important part of pastoral care. With the other curate (with whom I had been at King's College London with, but he was two years ahead of me) we ran the young people's group, organised a few 'youth services' and even one for the diocese in the cathedral – an all-night vigil with workshops etc, ending with an early morning Eucharist. I played the organ for youth services in the parish, for the one above in the cathedral, and sometimes helped the organist out if there were more weddings on one day than he could manage (the most we had on one Saturday was five). I deputised for the precentor at the cathedral when he had a day off by singing choral evensong.

My second curacy was in a benefice with two parishes and churches. The vicar and I had known each other since I was a teenager when he was a curate at our parish church, and he knew my family well. The work on Epsom Downs was very similar to Rainham with the services and pastoral care but the difference was the racecourse and its attendant organisation and people – travellers especially around Derby week added to the numbers of population and brought with them a different culture and way of life from the usual inhabitants of the parish. I did a number of funerals for the racing fraternity – even having a life-size horse made of flowers for a service at the crematorium.

I think both curacies helped me with priestly formation and pastoral care but unlike today there was little or no post-ordination training (as it was called) from the diocese. In my title parish I did see a tutor from time to time who asked me to write an essay, and a canon from the cathedral gathered us together occasionally for a day conference. Towards the end of my second curacy the bishop mentioned looking for a parish because he had one in mind. Although I had been ordained for nearly six years, I was rather nervous about the responsibility of running a parish. A chance advertisement in the *Church Times* for chaplains in the Royal Navy and meeting a retired bishop who had been a chaplain in the RN during the war, encouraged me to look into the possibility. My wife had been a nursing sister in the RN Queen Alexandra's Royal Naval Nursing Service (QARNNS) when I first met her while still a student. After an initial interview with the chaplain of the fleet and a familiarisation visit to Portsmouth Naval Base and ships with chaplains, I was offered a post as chaplain RN which lasted sixteen years and included a variety of experiences in ships, submarines, naval hospitals and training establishments. In this respect I was not involved in parochial ministry as such although ministering in the RN was very akin to the demands on life as a priest and pastor. We saw each ship or establishment as 'our parish', and much of the pastoral work was done with families who were living ashore. Towards the end of my sixteen years, in spite of pressure to stay, I felt I really should return to parochial ministry in all its fullness.

Parish Then and Now

I was fortunate to be offered the living of Tavistock with Gulworthy on leaving the RN by the Bishop of Exeter. A vibrant town parish with a small country one with no village as such but small farming communities dotted throughout. But for all that Gulworthy had a lively congregation who appeared weekly from the surrounding area. As well as the Sunday services there was a keen group who organised social gatherings regularly.

The town parish of Tavistock was once described to me as a quintessentially English parish. In 1992 when I became incumbent there was an electoral roll of well over 300. Attendance was good – 8.00 am holy communion (HC) 25, 9.45 am sung Eucharist 150, sung Evensong 30, and on festivals and special occasions there were considerably more. The church could seat 400, and we had a very competent organist and choirmaster with a choir of 30. There was morning and evening prayer with a daily Eucharist. We had an average of 100 funerals a year, mostly in church, with some seventy baptisms and thirty weddings. The church was in the square in the middle of the town surrounded by the town hall, magistrates' court and Bedford Hotel with the vicarage next door. The church was used by the community for many activities, concerts and flower festivals. There were two Church schools which used the building regularly, and all five other schools and colleges used the church for their special occasions. It was very much a civic church, and it was said that the two people who would be seen at any town event were the mayor and the vicar. There were also alms-houses for which the vicar was automatically a trustee, and chair of governors of the church schools. The vicar was also chaplain to the local hospital which at the time had in-patients as well as clinics, outposts of the main hospital in Plymouth. I was also chaplain to Kelly College, the local independent school and eight years a governor of College of St Mark and St John in Plymouth (now Marjon University).

Tavistock was known as a 'training parish' and there was a stipendiary deacon in post when I arrived who was later ordained priest when that became possible. Her husband, a retired schoolteacher, was also a priest and was a Self-Supporting Minister (SSM) curate. Over the years I had five curates in training who moved onto their own livings. There were also two Melanesian Brothers who came to me for a year at the request of their bishop to gain experience of an English parish, one of whom is now archbishop of Melanesia, the other sadly died while being mission secretary of the Anglican Church of Melanesia. There were also four retired clergy who had PTO living in the parish and who were able to assist with some services for me and other parishes nearby.

Today

Now my third successor has six parishes to cover, something which is common across the board in English dioceses. Much of what was considered normal parochial ministry has changed. It was once said that a 'house-going parson led to a Church-going people'. Now pastoral response has to be according to need, often only in urgent need. There are also many, some would say, that it is a lack of belief, that faith is now no longer part of life for many, and that the secular ideologies have replaced them. Covid certainly had its effect on numbers, and some have never returned to Sunday worship in church who were once regulars before the pandemic. There is also what I would call the trivialisation of life and death. The adverts on TV for Pure Cremation say quite plainly, no one wants an expensive funeral these days. Facing the reality of death, grief and bereavement seem to be swept under the carpet.

However, I cannot subscribe to the merchants of gloom and despondency. I believe the parish system can still be a very positive part of our nation's life. Someone said to me a few years ago that what we need is a slimmer and fitter Church. There are examples of great commitment and of new and enterprising initiatives which reflect the mission of the Church in different ways and include much interaction with the community. Churches being reordered to accommodate community activities, doctors' surgeries, Post Offices and other enterprising essentials. The Church showing a welcome and working to accommodate the needs of those around will not necessarily bring in masses of new congregations, but the goodwill demonstrated and care for people and their needs helps them to realise that the Church is there for them when they need help. Food banks, dementia groups and addiction groups have all been given space and volunteers from churches. Covid also brought out a lot of good things in the way clergy came to grips with new IT skills and bringing 'Church' into people's homes. Some are still finding live streaming services effective, especially for those who cannot physically be present in the church building. There is also the fact that often when tragedies occur, both local and national, clergy are seen on TV speaking about what has occurred and the human response to what happened. The Church still has a place in national life and people turn to it to express grief and light candles. In many places there has been growth in ecumenical and interfaith working together to alleviate local needs and share in worship. Lay people are being given greater scope to offer their own ministries and being made to feel they have a proper place in the life of the Church, and not just as the vicar's helpers. Some have proved great skill in leading lay led services which have become more frequent as the numbers of clergy available have declined. There are also the retired clergy who outnumber the stipendiary clergy by a large proportion. In this diocese we have over 300 many of whom have PTO and offer a great service to the parishes. There are also societies which help clergy maintain their equilibrium and avoid the burn out which is always a possibility with the added demands and stresses they have to face. The Sheldon Community is doing some great work in this respect and for those of a particular churchmanship the Society of Catholic Priests (SCP) allows clergy to find support, inspiration and encouragement. Similarly, the Retired Clergy Association offers opportunity to meet, worship and have some relevant input to assist in their ministry. Our group meets monthly for the Eucharist, socialising and often a talk by a theological educator or writer. The diocese has contributed financially in recent years to assist with fees/expenses which has been much appreciated. When we retire from parochial ministry, we put aside the organisational aspects of running a parish but still value being able to exercise the ministry for which we were ordained. Once a priest always a priest.

Finally, there is the worship itself. Recent years have witnessed an increase in cathedral attendance. This may have something to do with anonymity, but I think more to do with the quality of the liturgy, music and preaching etc. Most parish churches cannot imitate cathedrals, but they can ensure that what is offered is the very best which they can produce. 'That's all right, it is only for the church', is an attitude which is anathema to me. If we are known to be attempting to make the best of the resources that we have in any place for the glory of God and the building up of the community of the faithful and the 'unsure' adherent, we shall be given the increase, but that may be very different from what we expect. God is a God of surprises. We are called to be faithful not successful. Let God do the rest.

Editorial Comment: This contributor has raised several interesting and pertinent points. Being a chaplain in the military forces, hospitals, education, prisons and so forth may not be parish life, but it is part of priesthood, and it has many similarities and impacts as parish life. His reflections on his training and experience as a curate may be in sharp contrast to what happens today, and his response to the change of life in terms of numbers attending, the increase of parishes under one priest, the use of Church buildings for community use, the value of retired clergy, these factors are all positive. This must all be kept in mind as we continue to search for what is happening in today's parish life.

The Revd. Douglas Robertson

The Revd. Douglas Robertson: Deacon in 2007, priested in 2008. I trained part-time at the South-East Institute of Theological Education from 2004 to 2007. I was a stipendiary curate in the parish of Rochester in Kent from September 2007 to January 2011. My training incumbent was an excellent parish priest, and I was given lots of responsibility and led the ministry to the schools in the parish. Many of my contemporaries were also curates on a stipendiary basis, and as such were in training six days a week for three or four years. There were also those who were on an NSM or SSM basis, making themselves available for a significant amount of time each week.

Recently there has been a significant reduction in the number of stipendiary curacies, and often those appointed as curates can only give a very limited amount of time to the Church. Consequently, it follows that their training is far from comprehensive, and training in and experience of pastoral ministry is adversely affected. I have offered to give experience of ministry in a rural setting to a curate training in an urban setting.

My incumbency was from February 2011 to November 2018 and was in a large village on the edge of Tunbridge Wells. It was a single parish, with two churches, and I was assisted by two readers, two PAs, two retired clergy, and for last three years a SSM curate. I retired after major surgery and moved to Malton.

Current Parish System In My Area

I am now rector of the Howardian group benefice, consisting of five village communities in a rural setting, but united as one benefice. I came out of retirement in 2022 to become half-time stipendiary rector on a rolling one/two-year basis because I am now over 70. Each village in my benefice has a strong identity and the Church is an important element in the life of those villages, even though the percentage of villagers attending worship on a regular basis is low. However, major festivals such as Harvest and Christmas, are well supported, and funerals are regularly held in each church. Marriages are less frequent because of competition from venues that can host both the ceremony and the reception.

When I was appointed, I felt that it was important to visit pastorally and to re-connect with the two primary schools and one prep school in my benefice. During the prior long vacancy those two aspects had been neglected.

It is far harder to be incumbent of five village communities than it is to be incumbent of a single parish, principally because of the lack of support (though I do have help from a priest with PTO). It is hard to recruit church wardens and PCC members, and finance is a significant issue. My own benefice understands that you get what you pay for, and they pay much more than my half-stipend.

Some of My Observations

We have a very good area dean and lay dean. I find the Archdeacon of York to be very helpful, as was the previous Bishop of Selby, but I have yet to meet the new bishop. There is a lot emanating from the diocese, such as material relating to its 'rhythm of life'. It is good material but also an uphill struggle to encourage parishes to take it up. For me, there is insufficient understanding that the pastoral ministry on the ground is vital. 'People don't care what you know until they know you care'. This means that we need more people with dog collars on the ground.

There now seems to be a disconnect between the diocese and the many parishes in rural locations. There is a widespread feeling that there are too many managers in the diocesan office, and not enough clerical positions on the frontline where it counts. There is also a feeling that, nationally, senior Church leaders are trying to instil management procedures more suited to a large public company than a caring church.

It is very hard to fill vacancies in our deanery. The house for duty no longer appears attractive, and many parishes/benefices are unable to fund even a half stipend. Bearing this factor in mind, joint appointments with the Methodist Church may become more common. So much time is taken up in PCC meetings with issues relating to the upkeep of their Church buildings. These buildings are part of our national heritage and perhaps the state should take some responsibility for them, as in France and other European countries. We feel almost backward, not one of my churches has a toilet. This is a problem, especially regarding weddings and funerals. How good it would be if each church had a toilet and facilities for the disabled, a demand which must be met in many secular buildings.

There is a need for more lay ministers. I have three gentlemen who are willing to lead morning and evening prayer on a regular basis. The more lay ministers we have the more services we will be able to have in our churches. Maintaining the continuity of worship in each church is essential.

Attendances fell following the Covid pandemic, but they have started picking up again. Unfortunately, there are so many other attractions, particularly for children, especially on Sundays. However, Church attendance should not be the main criterion for the success of a church. For example, I know that my churches are used as places of private prayer, one is used to host the village coffee mornings, as God's house must be seen as open for his people.

Editorial Comment: This contributor has drawn attention to the fact that in his setting the rural church is still the focus for many funerals which is good, and this raises the question as whether this has something to do with the more peaceful rural setting. He also underlined the importance of visiting, not least the parish schools which is critical in a parish priest's ministry. Like so many others he noted that looking after five and not one parish can be more of a burden. It is fortunate that priesthood is a vocation and not career post, as this would lead to strikes and demands for extra pay. This aspect leads onto his understandable criticism that from the top echelons of church leadership come demands for secular type management, noting also the number of posts in diocesan houses. He ends on a positive note that keeping the churches open by making them available for the local community's activities, even if just coffee mornings, is ongoing and critical as God's house is open to all. This editor can recall a time when a coffee morning was held in his church, and a young man asked why he bowed every time he crossed the aisle. The reply that it was built as God's house, and his presence was acknowledged by the crucifix on the altar produced a small laugh. A week later the same man came to a service and three months later was a regular member of the congregation, volunteering to mow the grass in the graveyard.

The Revd. Tim Wright

I am the Revd. Tim Wright BD AKC and was made deacon in June 1964 and ordained priest the year after. I am middle of the road in my views, seeing the Eucharist as central for worship. I read theology at King's College London, and was trained for ministry at St Boniface College, Warminster which consisted of lectures on pastoral topics and taking services in local parish churches.

I spent four years as a curate in Headington, Oxford, before going into schools to become a school chaplain and later a housemaster and headmaster. My experience as a parish priest is limited, although I have always helped in parishes where I have been based. There was a strong tradition of visiting the houses in the parish in my curacy which succeeded in giving the impression that the Church cared for everyone and was appreciated. This tradition has been mostly abandoned in recent times for many reasons, and the local churches now seem to prioritise their worshippers.

Today there now appears to be a more inward-looking approach from the parish clergy, with the intention of maintaining the regular congregation, although some clergy try hard to become involved in local events so that they are seen and recognised. In this way they are showing themselves as custodians of the local church and find support when the church holds events. People, especially in rural areas, identify with their local church even though they are not regular worshippers. This is an aspect of the parish system which is valuable and needs to be maintained and used.

There certainly is a decline in church attendance and one of the reasons, in my view, is that church going is not seen as an attractive option. Services are often drab with the same old ritual which does not excite people used to more stimulating events in the secular world. The book of common worship offers a choice of eucharistic services which should be used with music of good quality.

Our Church leadership wastes its time on a pedantic, legalistic approach to safeguarding and on popular issues of the day like feminism or reparation for slavery. Naturally, these are important and must always been borne in mind, but the Church should first and foremost be trying to encourage and nurture faith. There are a lot of people who have a residual faith who do not attend church, and we are not reaching out to them. Our Church leaders are not developing ways to identify and attract such people. They come across as more negative such as issues of same sex marriage, and they seem out of touch with the ordinary work of the parish church. They should be leading us to become a friendly community, welcoming everyone and making them feel valued. I am inclined to say that all the dressing up with mitres and capes, cassocks and chasubles does not help, although I personally like such things as they give a sense of occasion. I am certain, though, that we should be an inclusive body welcoming everyone without rules or restrictions. This seems to me essentially trying to be like Christ and, unfortunately, our Church leaders do not come across as such, although some parish priests manage this critical approach.

In my opinion the parish system is there to be used. It has tradition behind it, which is widely accepted and understood, but bypassing it with extraneous appointments at a diocesan level undermines this and wastes money.

Editorial Comment: In this brief contribution the writer raises some important questions which cannot be ignored. The old parish priest tradition of visiting people in their homes is becoming rarer by the day, and this has a direct impact on his next point of today's clergy being more concerned about 'maintaining their regular congregation'. A congregation eventually dies off by sheer old age, and it needs new people. In days gone by this used to be achieved by visiting and serving the community, a point raised by many other contributors. He also makes the important point that for many the local church is not just an odd edifice but is viewed by many people as 'their church', in so far that it helps identify their community. It is well known that people who offer to help maintain their church as a community offering, frequently become worshippers. The contributor also draws attention to the management level of the church authorities being more concerned about legalistic issues such as safeguarding and apologising for the twist and turns of past history. On a recent visit to Samoa both King Charles III and the prime minister kept explaining they could not be responsible for the moral conduct of past generations in terms of slavery. Finally, again in common with many others, he raises the question of the number of diocesan house appointments when the parish churches are suffering from a shortage of clergy. Without the work of the parish the Church may soon become a cathedral-based organisation for special national ceremonial occasions.

The Revd. Angela Reynolds

As a summary of my background, I moved to Norfolk and was ordained deacon in 1997 and priested a year later, retiring in 2009 and still helping with a PTO. I was brought up in the Church of England from birth, my father was a lay reader in the Southwark diocese and later ordained in St Paul's Cathedral when he was 50. In terms of worship, I am traditional middle of the road, and I did my theological training with the East Anglian ministerial training course, during which I continued as a lay reader while in our seventeen-parish rural benefice. During my training I had placements at Thorpe St Andrew Hospital (psychiatric and old people), Norfolk and Norwich Hospital chaplaincy and St Elizabeth's parish, Earlham, where the parish priest had recently died, but his wife a city councillor took me on and organised my placement.

I felt called to full time ministry, not necessarily stipendiary. Sadly, I was sent back by the Bishop of Lynn to be NSM curate in the parishes in which I lived, as a female incumbent had been appointed while I was training, and whom I believe had some influence in my appointment back into the group where I had been worshipping for over twenty-three years. This meant I did not receive the wider liturgical experience I would have valued, but I was well versed in parish workings and village life having served on Easton Parish Council before we moved a few villages away, I was a WI president, secretary at various times, and a PCC secretary of the small parish in which we lived, as well as taking over as group secretary in the Barnham Broom and Upper Yare group and deanery synod secretary for a short time. After eighteen months of my curacy, I was offered the post of interim priest-in-charge of the benefice of Easton, Colton and Marlingford under the guidance of a mentor which gave me the experience and responsibility of full parish ministry. I met with my mentor, a retired parish priest, every month or so, the idea at the time was to work with the neighbouring parish, but this never happened as the priest retired through ill health, and the parish still has no priest. The church warden does not like women priests, but the parish share was always paid. My curacy obviously did not take the usual route, and after my three-year curacy concluded, I was made priest-in-charge and another parish was added, I was given a half-stipend but eventually received the full amount.

Having worshipped and ministered in a benefice of many parishes as a lay person, a lay reader then a curate it was a very happy experience, and we saw how this number of parishes could work together successfully with the goodwill of the people. The parishes worked together in pairs for worship each with their own PCC. Eventually a group council was formed which met every quarter which helped divide the group share between the parishes. At the time each parish had at least one church warden and most had two plus various church officers. Some parishes had a small population living in the village and although the attendance was not great the Church was supported and was part of the village life and community. PCCs met infrequently in people's homes (warmer), or informally at the back of the church and AGMs were held annually. On the fifth Sundays a group service was held which brought together congregations from the group churches with coffee afterwards, usually in a local large house or the back of the church. A few churches had gradually built on a small kitchen and toilets, but the heating then was either non-existent or by radiant heating from wall heaters, a few had gas cylinder heaters, but we all knew we had to dress warmly when meeting in a church. A team of eight lay readers was established, and we were given permission by Bishop Graham James to take extended communion, so the parishes were covered at special festivals. Each Parish attempted to pay their allocated share and building repairs.

I personally feel that the parish system in rural areas is extremely important for the local community, and when in post I regarded non-church goers as part of my 'cure of souls' and seeing the church and village as one. As the parish priest, I went into the local schools and was a governor of one, I went to the local parish council meetings to show interest (and sometimes fell asleep for which I was teased) and attended as many fetes and village events as possible. These links encouraged church attendance on special occasions and meant that in each village the Church had a visible presence. Members of other denominations were also welcomed as they grew older, or the chapel closed, and they could no longer attend their own church. Each parish had their own treasurer and fabric officer, but they were not necessarily regular members of the congregation. I was very well supported by my husband who was a reader before I was, and he still is.

I appreciate that as more and more parishes are being grouped together it is difficult for one person to carry out a similar ministry, but in the villages there are people living in them with great gifts who can be encouraged to use them and make the role of 'the vicar' easier, but it requires a willingness on the part of the priest to let go of certain tasks, become more flexible and develop a feeling for and acceptance of people as they are, with their likes and dislikes of different liturgies, and by encouraging the gifts of the less confident and using the wisdom of those with experience. I firmly hold to the idea that if a church needs large repairs the money can be found from various grants, and our diocese offers help with form filling and other matters. Attendance might be falling but nobody wants a church to close, which demands imagination on the part of the congregation, the village as a whole, clergy, and maybe the senior clergy of the diocese working in partnership with prayer, willingness to accept new ideas and compromises, commitment and openness, and listening and hearing those on the ground who know how neighbouring villages could work together which would revive the Church and increase a sense of Christian community.

Editorial Comment: This contributor has outlined her training and experience and reflects life in a rural-type setting. She has served in local secular posts, as a lay reader, a priest, and reflects a person with much knowledge of the demands of local rural life. She has rightly noted that a parish priest attends as many local functions, fetes and other local gatherings as possible, thereby implying the importance of the parish priest being seen as part of the community. She makes the interesting point that where some of the non-conformist chapels are struggling and closing, their members are turning to the parish churches which have remained opened. This has proved true in many areas, where Christians may have lost their buildings but remained united in their faith and where old denominational differences must be cast aside. She also has made the pertinent point that in the rural area no one wants the local parish church to close, which also, she points out, needs 'the goodwill of the people'.

Finally, she concludes with the major points that we must pull together, those at the ground level to the ecclesiastical hierarchy, and concludes with the telling line that 'listening and hearing those on the ground who know how neighbouring villages could work together would revive the Church'. This is an important statement that those who administer and lead the Church at the highest level should listen to the frontline officers and people who have firsthand experience of the emerging problems.

The Venerable Peter Lock

I was ordained deacon at Rochester Cathedral in 1968 and priested there in 1969. I remained in the diocese for the whole of my ministry. I had two curacies which lasted a total of eight years and then three incumbencies, and I finally served as archdeacon of Rochester which combined with a residential canonry at the cathedral where I was also a member of the dean and chapter. My parish ministry ranged from large spread-out Kent villages to a housing estate, to town centre churches. I was chair of the diocesan house of clergy for three years, and a member of the General Synod for twenty years. I retired in 2009. I would describe myself as a modern/liberal catholic.

My Training

I was trained at King's College London and St Boniface Warminster (1964–1968). The course was one which encouraged questioning and took biblical criticism seriously. It also included the study of philosophy and comparative religions and learning NT Greek. I would also include as influential in my thinking and faith the part played by my parish church where I was a chorister from the age of 8 and server, and where the clergy had a strong spiritual life, were thoughtful and inspiring preachers and regularly visited both those within and those outside the Church. I did not come from a church-going family but one which was enormously supportive when I started as a chorister. I received valuable pastoral support from the Church when my mother died when I was 14. Alongside my local church my school had a very active Christian Union (CU) whose basis was evangelical and where I eventually became leader. This gave me the opportunity to rub shoulders with boys of other Christian traditions and argue about theology in an informal way. The CU held a camp every summer in Devon which I know shaped boys lives and produced even one or two bishops, as well as leaders of other denominations.

Experience as a Curate

I was married three months before I was ordained as a deacon as I had known my then girlfriend for eight years, and we wanted to start ordained life together as a married couple. The Bishop of Rochester (David Say) suggested that we should marry after leaving theological college, and then I would start at our parish as a licensed lay worker for three months and be paid as such before I was ordained in the Michaelmas 1968. So straight after our honeymoon we arrived at the parish. This was not the normal arrangement, but it worked for us. We had a lovely basic three-bedroomed semi-detached house with no central heating. The church was middle-of-the road but very outward looking and engaged with the community. I had a great vicar who was both friendly and instructive. He gave of himself and worked long hours which probably cost him his marriage. It was a sacrificial ministry. He expected the same from me.

The church community welcomed us warmly and we remained in contact with some of the people there throughout our ministry. Many of them also were young married couples. But the church had a wide range of age groups. I recall that even then my wife was not expected to be 'the unpaid curate' but could pursue her own career if she wanted.

Post ordination training was not onerous but enjoyable all the same. I recall studying Ephesians, having a lecture from a leading psychiatrist, and studying and writing an essay on Dietrich Bonhoeffer. I do not recall completing a ministry review with the vicar or anyone else as happens nowadays. Although I would have had informal conversations about my ministry with the vicar. Whilst I was given free reign about involvement with the community I was expected to visit regularly and was given lists of roads as well as people to see. I remember being told by someone that as a priest you would be about the only person who could cold call and be given a welcome, which is probably not so nowadays.

My involvement with young people included helping to run the village youth club in my first curacy, and I was trained by Kent County Council as a part-time youth leader whilst there. I was expected to plan and undertake the confirmation course for young people. In terms of the pastoral offices, they were considered a vital aspect of ministry. I was soon visiting couples who had enquired of baptism for their children, and I was expected to be at their monthly preparation course, as well as take the baptism service in an afternoon. There would usually be at least three families per month. There were also plenty of weddings, some on the same day. I would usually take about twelve a year and the vicar a similar number. There were plenty of funeral services, sometimes two on the same day. Thankfully I never had to do a crematorium duty.

On reflection, I was grateful that I had two curacies. All incumbents were inspirational, supportive and expected a lot from young curates. Preaching was to be a thoughtful and intelligent presentation of the gospel. There was a great emphasis on pastoral care not only of the congregation but also of people outside the church. They were not afraid to be quite radical in their approach. I undertook one interregnum which I think helped me further develop my ministry. In total I was just over eight years as a curate before I came to my first incumbency. I consider myself fortunate that it was this long and with clergy who were well-trained themselves.

Parish System Yesterday and Today

Pastoral offices were important as they brought you into contact with all sorts of people – it was the mainstay of mission, but now in serious decline. Today many marriages are now conducted by the state. Hospital visiting was also important, visiting whoever was in hospital at the time whether or not they were Church of England. Data protection has put an end to this practice.

The seasons of the Christian year also gathered in a few outsiders: Harvest, Christmas, Easter (less so) Mothering Sunday (more so). Remembrance Sunday also saw parades with which the church was involved. There were school assemblies on a regular basis, especially primary schools who also came to church for Christmas. I was also a school governor in my second curacy and from then onwards in every parish I was a governor of at least one school. I was also a chairman three times.

We did not have to deal with safeguarding (maybe we should have taken this more seriously, but I think we left clergy discipline to the bishops). Liturgically we had to be alert because there were many revisions of the BCP, such as Series 1, 2 and 3, the Alternative Service Book (ASB) and finally common worship throughout my ministry. This also caused a loss of a daily office as there was not one easily available with readings etc. When I was first ordained the daily office had possibly an unseen but profound effect on the clergy. For many the weekly BCP office was by now tired and lifeless.

Some of the major pastoral tussles were over the (second) marriage of divorced people, on the question of the baptism of infants, and how to prepare parents and godparents was important, with the blessing of infants being encouraged when parents did not attend church. As problems these seem small beer now.

Decline in Church Membership

There can be no doubt that society has itself changed radically over the last fifty years. It is not only about adjusting to the new technologies and the change in living patterns like Sunday trading. There are fewer people attending church, fewer young people and families, more questioning the Christian faith and more willing to say they are atheists. Some have become more strident in their criticism of the faith as well as the Church. The Humanist Society is more active and vocal. I do not think the church answered the Richard Dawkins of this world with any great conviction or commitment, partly because the evangelical wing of the Church of England became more fundamentalist and strident in its biblical attitude.

Safeguarding issues and the way the Church has (or has not) dealt with this has not helped the church's public image. Both Roman Catholic and Anglican churches have suffered from this as well as the rise of Islamic fundamentalism, which has created a backlash against 'religion' in general.

Of course, there have been the courses like 'Alpha' that have been popular mostly among evangelical churches and have drawn in the middle classes. But in many of the smaller, middle of the road type churches it has been a case of the 'faithful few fighting bravely'. They, mainly the elderly, have attempted to maintain both ministry, mission and maintenance faithfully and not always appreciated. Funding of ancient buildings is an issue which causes both stress and anxiety when hundreds of thousands of pounds have to be raised to repair a listed building. If the current government decides to end the scheme whereby VAT can be reclaimed on repairs to listed places of worship, then further additional monies will need to be raised.

However, all in all, I think the problem is not one of finance but of faith. The Church now has to live, teach as well as preach the faith in ways which the current generations can understand and freshly experienced.

Locked doors as well as locked minds in the Church will not help. Being open to the world will.

Editorial Comment: This contributor who started his training and ministry some sixty years ago raises some interesting insights. The first was the importance of post ordination training mentioned in the article on ordination training, and as with many others the critical nature of visiting in the parish. He also reminds us of the many changes which have taken place in the liturgical formats of worship, and the essential nature of the pastoral offices, where we are all aware today of the decline of church weddings, lack of baptisms and the increasing number of humanists conducting funerals. He dwells on the loss of faith raising the issue of not 'answering the Richard Dawkins of this world', as there are many persuasive intellectual arguments to challenge this viewpoint. This is an issue which still needs addressing, starting with the basic question of asking 'why is there something and not nothing' and 'what and who are we?' Perhaps it is time to be more open and be prepared to challenge the 'locked doors as well as locked minds in the Church' and be open with Christian witness and persuasion.

Chapter Three

Lay Person's Response

Introduction

A lay person when defined in the dictionary indicates someone who is not an expert or professional in a certain field or activity. In terms of church life, it demands a slight shift of emphasis. The dictionary is correct is so far that a lay person within the church structure is usually defined as not ordained and cannot lead a sacramental service but can assist with the bishop's permission. Fifty years ago, the leading lay figures tended to be lay readers allowed to preach, with selected Bible readers at the lectern. Lay people also included PCC members ranging from treasurers to secretary or record keepers, those running the Sunday school and youth clubs. By the 1970s it was common practice for selected lay people to be chalice bearers and as the years have passed their function has dramatically increased and they often lead worship, and some do pastoral visiting. Again, technically, anyone who is not ordained is a lay person, but for this research a lay person is a congregational member who assists the parish priest at any level of parish work, from assisting in or taking services, helping run the Church as PCC members, or in a myriad of posts many created locally. Normally a parish priest is not trained in accountancy, book-keeping and management, and a lay person trained in these skills plays not only a supportive role but a critical one freeing the priest to do what he/she was trained and called for, the caring and cure of souls and worship of God. The shortage of clergy has clearly made the work of such lay people much more important, and now the priest often has many more churches to care for, they have become much more critical which is why their views are so important in this project.

During the last fifty or so years there has been a major change in the way lay people are perceived and in how they perceive themselves. In the past it was likely that an active lay person in the Church would see their contribution as a matter of assisting or supporting the vicar. Now they are more likely to see their work as a distinctive and valid form of ministry in its own right. There has been much encouragement for them to do this, chiefly on the basis of St Paul's teaching about the body of Christ with its 'many limbs and organs'. No one could possibly argue that this is anything other than a healthy development, but it does raise some issues. We often speak of lay leaders and use phrases like, 'every member ministry', but there is a need to work out how this relates to the role of the ordained priest. How does the growth in lay ministry affect the role of the ordained priest in the parish? What form of leadership is expected from the incumbent?

This issue has particular importance in areas where ordained clergy are in short supply. In many small rural parishes, there is often a highly dedicated lay individual who in reality leads the local church. This can cause problems when the ordained minister, who has theoretical charge of the parish, is seldom present and has less knowledge of the parish, its history and its residents than the lay people.

Perhaps the key to what sort of leadership the clergy need to provide is service. There was a certain parish priest some years ago who said it was his job to keep 'the laos in their topos'. This reflected an antiquated view that the vicar was the ultimate authority about everything. It has its equivalent in a phrase sometimes heard in Roman Catholic churches when someone says, 'Father knows best'. Thankfully we have moved a long way from this sort of thinking, but there is a need to think about how lay and ordained serve together.

Maurice Keys

My name is Maurice Keys, a longtime lay reader currently in Southampton in the Winchester diocese. I was born in the baby boomer generation and grew up in the 1960–1970 years, with attending church being an important and focal part of my life. During that period, I attended a church which one could describe as middle-of-the road and one located in what would be described as an urban village in a city setting because it was its own parish. My early education was at the local church infant's school. In those days I recall visits to the church during school days on those days of importance and celebration.

As my education progressed, I sensed a diluting of contact between school and church. So that by the time I reached secondary school the only connections with faith at school would have been bi-weekly school assemblies, which involved a singing of a hymn and having a Bible lesson read, and a visit to the local parish church for a Christmas carol service. After sixth form college I left the area to work in London pursuing a career as a civil servant from which I have just retired.

My experience of the parish church in London was the distinctive style of churchmanship with which I was already familiar, as it was what we called high church, and the liturgy and language were similar. My area of London, although affluent, had a transient and multicultural population and for the time I was there, it was friendly, but it felt different. I can recall the priest being the only person who really engaged with me, and I never got to know any of the real congregation. Later, I moved to another part of London and once again moved to a parish which was high church which was forward in faith. Compared to the earlier parish I found this a distinct experience being more involved in the Church and parish life. This church was essentially run by one priest but assisted by readers and church army personnel. After a number of years in London I returned to my original parish in Southampton to deal with a number of family issues.

Following my return home, I started training as a reader and was licenced in 2003. The return to my home parish saw a number of changes in both personnel and congregation. During my growing years, the area had relied heavily on local industry and commerce. However, after an absence of twenty-five years most of that industry was either gone or in decline. The local naval shipyard had been replaced by a small housing estate whose people seemed to have no contact with the long-standing residents of the parish. A priest not allocated to the parish was assigned to that community, described as a pioneering minister. The process failed to make any meaningful connections with that community or our parish, meaning our parish and the new estate still co-exist as seemingly separate entities.

I mentioned that a number of the congregation had changed since I returned, and whilst congregations change over time, I often wonder if it were the socio-economic changes had any influence in this. After the Second World War Britain was changing: people were staying in education longer (my parents left school at 14 years of age). By the 1960s and 1970s, people were leaving home to go to university and to take on careers which would take them away from home, and families were becoming widespread. A lot of people went away and never came back to their home church, but I often wonder whether they kept their faith by attending another church or drifted away. Other variations in the area were the cultural changes with other faiths arriving. Today, one only has to look at the local shopping area to see how outside influences have changed the place of my youth. Whereas in the 1960s to the 1970s shops were closed on a Sunday, which is now a normal shopping day if not the main day for this pursuit. I often wonder how the Church can survive with so many outside influences or how it can adapt.

Looking back, I feel that the clergy during the 1960–1970 era had more respect than they seem to have nowadays. I base this view on the response I see as a reader today. For one example, on occasions I have assisted my parish priest at baptisms where I greet people coming into church and provide them with an order of service and guide them where to sit. On performing this duty, I am met with a major change in response by those coming for the service. The more elderly visitors enter quietly, politely, and reverentially while the younger generations enter church with a vastly different demeanour. They are as a rule, less quiet and often address me as: 'hi mate', or 'watch-ya vic'. Because I wear a cassock, surplice and the reader's scarf they assume that I am the vicar. I point out to them that I am not the vicar, and I do not wear a dog collar.

In the more recent years because of the reductions in parish finances and loss of clergy numbers, in many parishes included mine, we must share incumbents. This arose because those originally allocated one parish are now finding themselves managing two parishes or more. From a lay perspective the parish responses to these directives are interesting. People who grew up in one church environment are sometimes reluctant to go to a neighbouring parish to worship, because they feel the style of worship is not to their liking. In our example the priest taking the service is the same and the order of service is only 'slightly' different. There is however a significant reluctance to travel between the neighbouring parishes, as many see the home parish as their home, rightly or wrongly.

Another concern the congregation feels is that on some Sundays the main morning service is one of the word rather than one of Eucharist. This has raised concerns as many of the elderly members want to receive communion every Sunday. They sometimes respond that when having a reader taking a service that they are missing their right to receive communion. Yet curiously, although the neighbouring parish offers the eucharist with their regular priest, they opt not to go there. For my part, I wonder whether this demeans the role of a reader in parish life. I think not, as the roles of a priest are quite different to those of a reader. It is all within the regulations and the orders of the episcopacy whose rules we must follow.

One cannot look at the Church as a whole over the past fifty years without looking at the way that it has managed its many changes, with dramas and dividing people. One of my initial thoughts in this area concerns the ordination of women priests with the legislation to allow them to become priests in November 1992. I am not raising the argument regarding this issue, but the way it was done. From a lay point of view, it was interesting to watch the many debates on both sides of the arguments. Undoubtedly many decisions were made with a great deal of prayer, and discussion, so I asked myself how this far-reaching decision affected secular observers. However, from my occupation in the secular world, many of my colleagues wondered how an organisation based on pastoral care and love could treat one another in such a way and with so much discord if not venom. There had been considerable vitriol and anger created by many who felt they had a calling and were being denied purely because of their gender. I can accept that at the end of the day a great deal was achieved, but conversely at what cost for the Church in England and our relations with our fellow Christians in communion around the world, and from non-church going cynical observers, but that is only my view.

On another issue which I think was significant were the ramifications of covid on our congregations. A time when it simply was not possible to come to church to share our faith and do what for generations, we had taken for granted. Being housebound was not a pleasant experience and one in which many people suffered. The Church also suffered in this instance. Services could be conducted by 'Zoom' or over 'the net', but on the return to church people were forced to sit apart to keep safe, making the church feel like a war zone. I had to ask myself, as to how can a place which is meant to be warm and welcoming be restrictive on numbers, when people can come in and be ordered where they must sit or stand. Strangely enough I have also received positive comments to this covid period where people could join in the service from home during covid, could sit and join in the service whilst eating breakfast, being in their pyjamas and getting their Sunday lunches ready; it provided a new form of outreach used to this day.

From a worshipping perspective it is interesting to see that at Christmas time we have Christingle services which attract families, and the church is packed with people, yet on Good Friday our service finds attendance rarely reaches above twenty people, and which from my spiritual point of view one could argue it is more important than Christmas.

To summarise my personal thoughts, I ask myself is the modern Church relevant to the people today. People still attend church, possibly not in the numbers of days gone by but there is still a faith at the coalface. There seems a serious decline in clergy and money issues remain dominant, but both clergy and laity have so much to offer and if they are given the opportunity to join in the conversation can help to shape the Church of the future. Perhaps the parish system which has worked so well for many years needs to change in some way. Hopefully, a way without conflict, but one of reinvention which is prayerful, practical, and relevant to the needs of God's people.

Editorial Comment: This contribution comes from a person of wide experience, who not only has noted the social and cultural changes in our society, but who has astutely observed changes within the parish system with the loss of clergy, their loss of respect, and even commenting on the changes in the role of the lay reader. He draws our attention to the problem of uniting different parishes and the problems from the congregational point of view. He also pointed out the issues created by the heated if not vitriolic debate around the ordination of women which did little to help the public views, and the way Covid was handled, as these debates were not only disruptive but hardly sent out the Christian message of love. He also added the divisions within the church can be equally as damaging. He demonstrated this issue by referring to where the emphasis is on 'the word' and not 'the Eucharist', implying the clash between the evangelical and Catholic inclined wing. We all worship our Lord in different ways, but it should not lead to hostility or division within the ranks, not least because, of once again, the failing image which undermines the relevance of the Church of God.

Lisa Lloyd

My name is Lisa Lloyd, a long-term church warden in a rural area of the Norwich diocese. I have been a regular long-term worshipper. In the past I have been church warden for approximately twenty years, the PCC secretary for eight. Although currently I am not a member of the PCC, I organise and take a major part in the following roles of heading up the fundraising and the social and refreshment team. I also organise and take a prominent role in rotas for readers and intercessors at Sunday services, as well as cleaning the church and tolling the bell for funerals. We are now in a team ministry of fourteen parishes with three priests in post, assisted, thankfully, by a few retired clergy, and parish AWAs. It is a fairly new arrangement but is well organised into three geographic groups covering all fourteen parishes and appears to be working well.

Our church has one Sunday communion service taken by the rector and two morning-prayer services each month, taken by AWAs, one Sunday each month we join another church in the group for holy communion. Finances are a constant worry as attendance is in decline, and those who attend are mostly 70 years and with some closer to 100 years old. The cost of living continually rises as does the parish share which does not make for a happy future.

In order of importance, I think the following are important in parish life: First, the parish priest should always wear a dog collar when out and about in the parish. Secondly, visits to dying and bereaved are for the priest but a trained lay team could help with sick visiting. Thirdly, leading services in each church of the group/benefice at least once during the month if other Sundays can be covered by AWAs. Fourthly, taking a moral stand is important to show the Church is aware of various issues. Finally, I think the group is too large for the old-fashioned visiting, but it is important for the parish priest to attend the village functions and talk to as many people as possible. In past years visiting had a marked effect on congregational growth.

Personally, I think the Church of England is on downward slope, even before Covid this was happening. I think the hierarchy of the Anglican Church appears totally ineffective; I am unaware of any serious initiative led by the current archbishop, although I gather, he is resigning as I ponder this work. I was shocked when he allowed churches to be locked during Covid, a time when solace in an empty church building which had stood open throughout the Black Death and the plague would have brought comfort.

For the Church to be effective it needs to be in touch with the people, currently it is not. I know I am old fashioned, but I feel that the loss of [Thomas] Cranmer's beautiful language in favour of the mediocre has been a big mistake. Exchanging the mystery for the mundane, has given the feeling that attendance at some church services is on a par with meeting friends in a coffee shop, which sadly, too often means intrigue, and any sense of spirituality can be lost.

I personally feel that there is little diocesan leadership that I am aware of, but I have to admit to being somewhat biased. Our church was in a well-organised, well-established benefice of three parishes when a few years ago a poorly educated, and inadequately trained incumbent was appointed. There seemed to be no diocesan guidance or leadership in place. The lady incumbent had little interest or knowledge of liturgy, a complete lack of empathy with small parish congregations, and next to no skill with people. Our identity as a worshipping community was lost as she omitted to arrange services for us, once leaving us without a service in our church for six weeks. The church wardens felt they should not rock the boat and would not complain so I did, but to no avail.

Both the then suffragan bishop and the archdeacon felt she was in their words, 'doing a good job', and I still have the archdeacon's letter of reply because I was so shocked. Our regular attendance fell away and of course once the habit of church going is lost it rarely returns. Fortunately, but only after six miserable years, that incumbent left, giving only three weeks' notice to the PCC. Currently our situation is a happy one, but it did not show the diocese in a good light.

Our current and excellent Incumbent who applied for the post of priest-in-charge of three parishes, discovered only at interview that the diocese had tacked on another two parishes making it up to five. Happily, for us she accepted the post when it was offered. However, I felt it showed a degree of shoddiness and arrogance on the part of the diocese. I was on that interviewing panel and subsequently on the panel for the next two posts in our team ministry. I discovered that the set of questions to interviewees insisted on by the diocese does not change and are so bland as to be useless.

On a positive note, to finish, our incumbent could not be better. She is extremely well organised and hardworking. She is an excellent communicator, very well educated and loves the church, takes time to prepare her teaching and cares for all the parishes. One excellent initiative she has up and running, is a Thursday 11.00 am communion service in our church every week.

People from all the different villages come and attendance is constantly between fourteen and twenty-four. I feel that this is very positive, and although it is not a Sunday when people might feel 'obliged' to come, they now make a positive choice to attend a mid-week communion service.

Editorial Comment: This contributor had been in a three-parish benefice which suddenly became fourteen. Just prior to the transition they had, in their estimation a poorly trained and difficult parish priest which the diocese ignored despite massive protests. The parishioners were worried about this priest, not least because church attendance rapidly dropped. When the next priest was appointed, it was for the parish a joy as she was hard working and dedicated. However, at the interviews she had applied for a benefice of three parishes only to discover during the actual interview that it had been enlarged to five, and this lay person expressed gratitude that the new priest accepted the post. However, all this resulted in deep criticism of the Church authorities at diocesan level. Naturally this contributor was also concerned about the constant demand for money and the challenge of Covid when the churches had been ordered to close. She pointed out that this had not happened during the Black Death and plague years, knowing something of the history of her locality. This dedicated contributor comes across as angry with the way the Church authority reacted to the parish dilemmas.

Canon Sir William Worsley

I am Canon Sir William Worsley, chapter member York Minster, also church warden and patron of All Saints Church Hovingham. I do not believe the rural church is in decline. We have been in interregnum for nearly four years and during our interregnum we have seen church numbers grow, in part because we are well served by wonderful, retired priests. A normal Sunday service in a small village has an attendance of around 20 with larger services having congregations of 80-100. The challenge is leadership, finance and an engagement with the rural church.

Our finances fall into two parts: maintaining the fabric of the church and funding the vicar and the Church of England. We do not spend all our time worrying about finances and over the years have had wonderful people leading our fundraising efforts. Finances are of course a challenge, but it is one step at a time and establishing the balance between building and Church.

I think the key role for a parish priest is to lead worship. The secondary role is visiting church goers at their time of need. Particularly visiting the sick, dying and bereaved. It is right to visit non-church goers, but this is dependent on time available. It is of course good for the vicar to be involved in community life, and this is not difficult to achieve. The key point is for them to be seen around and about.

I do not think the vicar should be a spokesperson for the whole community nor should be demanding of local politicians, making political stances. Personally, I am not bothered about the dog collar however it does mark the priest. The two key roles are leading worship and visiting those in need.

In some ways the Church is in decline. It has certainly not managed its finances well; however, the Church of England is a strange organisation, liberal, but it is as important now as ever. Indeed, all churches whether Methodist or Roman Catholic need to work much closer together and stop being 'silly'.

The key thing the Church needs is leadership, and this is largely lacking.

Editorial Comment: On this brief and succinct note from an active layman there was an immediate question as to whether the opening lines were deploying ironic humour, as he stated the rural church was not in decline, but they have had an 'interregnum for four years'. He noted that it was surviving and doing well mainly because of the help by retired clergy, which was good news, but marred by the knowledge that with *tempus fugit* in mind this hope is somewhat limited. With the drop in numbers of new clergy, the number of future retired clergy will reflect this problem. The good news is that his church is doing well because of the support of lay people which is critical as always. The editorial team agrees with his brief views on the role of the parish priest, with one small proviso which rarely arises, when local or national politicians step away from Christian morality and ethics. Most would agree that his views on interdenominational sharing makes sense, and this ecumenical move has started in some places. Like many others he concludes by questioning the role of Church leadership, but he has politely and correctly not made detailed points on this issue.

Jenny Lomas

I am Jenny Lomas, church warden for twenty years, now retired but continuing as a PCC member. The parish system has not adapted to the twenty-first century so far because it assumes that the laity volunteers have unlimited time to offer, as the local squire is no longer the church warden with unlimited time to give. Many church wardens and PCC members are in full-time working employment with a limited amount of time which they can offer to the Church. Those with more time tend to be retired, and sadly this often reflects the average age of the congregation with implications for a limited future. If there is no generation following the current parish then there will soon be an immediate risk for the future, unless the incumbent is forward looking, innovative, and pro-active, the future appears somewhat grim. Unfortunately, my current experience sees clergy taking a back seat and expecting the volunteers to do more than they are doing for any ongoing scheme, not just for a specific event. This affects morale in the parish and this downward spiral has not only started but is virtually established. I have noted that too many clergy give the impression that being a priest is a job rather than a vocation, and they are very conscious of the hours they work, which has become the general trend, but volunteers are expected to find the time on top of their normal work and home life.

The parish church is in decline, and to some extent this is parallel with other denominations experiencing similar problems as society has become more secular, but then why should people turn to a church which seems invisible, does not speak out at any level from parish upwards in any meaningful way to support their lives. I also feel the Church has become political in all the wrong ways. People feel ignored unsupported with no strong leadership to sustain their commitment in faith. The bishops and archbishops seem more concerned with business interests, their committees and seeking qualifications. While it may be important that there is a need for balance, people are not going to volunteer in great numbers if they need a certificate for everything. Bureaucracy is stifling growth, and if it continues it could bring about the collapse of the local churches.

Financially the expense of this is counterproductive, parishes fail to see why they should struggle to maintain buildings and pay quotas to support what we feel to be excessively overpaid officers and the advertisements for innumerable administrative posts. These seem to be more important than maintaining a Christian presence across the country.

A major problem would seem to be the way in which clergy are trained. Theology and Bible study are the basis of their faith, but running a parish in the twenty-first century requires much more, and these and other essential skills are too often sadly lacking. We have reached the point where poorly trained clergy are responsible for the training of curates, and consequently this factor further produces yet more weak leadership and management skills. This downward spiral is for me, as a long-term serving lay member, a matter of great concern.

If a PCC is the leadership in a parish, the vicar as chair should be the leader of the team, encouraging others and working with them, and sadly I see little of that these days, and consequently I am witnessing the crumbling of a once vibrant parish, and this disastrous momentum is happening from the very top. No one is expecting the vicar to be an expert in everything, but it is reasonable to assume that he or she would recognise the strengths of those in the congregation and encourage people to use them. A vicar should be using their own strengths and supporting others so that the parish works as a team with the vicar/rector/priest -in-charge having the guiding view. If this fails to happen then there is cause for apprehension for the future of the church and we should be concerned, I am certainly worried.

Editorial Comment: This lay contributor rightly points out that while the parish church has always depended on lay help, many are also busy in their lives and their time is limited. She also raises the worrying problem, as most are aware, that congregations are aging, so where is the next generation. Not surprisingly she points out the financial issues facing a parish and feel the top Church leadership to be ineffective.

Subsequently, she finds it annoying, noting that the leading figure should be the parish priest, but who generally tends to take a back seat. She noted that overall, our society has become more secular, which is right, and one of the opening articles explored this loss of faith. She then rapidly moves onto a point raised by many, that there are too many highly paid posts outside the parish all within the wider administration offices. She also raised the training of clergy which from her point of view has not been as efficient and as focused as in past years, and as these clergy instruct others the problem becomes ongoing.

Anonymous

I have held Church posts over the last few years. I have worked as a children and families' worker in south London, as a PCC member, a lead recruiter in the same area. More recently in Yorkshire I have been a parish safeguarding officer, member of the children's team, and, importantly, I would like to remain anonymous. Today in a small town in Yorkshire I play a part in my local benefice of which I have been a member for six years. The creation of the benefice happened a few years before I arrived, but it seems it was not a popular decision as far as most of the congregations were concerned. We shared a priest which has led to tensions over the last few years, as we are very different churches.

During recent years the local churches in our vicinity have relied on lay volunteers to lead an increasing number of activities, including worship, even when we had a vicar. These jobs often fall on women, and, due to time constraints, these are mainly retired women. Although we are lucky enough to have a few younger volunteers, as they all work full time and have busy family lives. Therefore, helping at church is a significant commitment, and I do not feel that it has been appreciated or supported by the vicar. In my opinion the parish priest's main task is to lead worship. However, while I believe that worship can be led by laity, it is very important for a parish priest to be there some of the time. I also believe that a parish priest should be involved in *all* [writer's emphasis] aspects of the parish-community life, making the Church community visible at all times. I prefer the old, traditional view of a parish priest going out to visit church goers and non-church goers alike, but I understand that this is not as easy now as it was in the past, not least because the priest's family dynamics have also changed with the times. I do believe, however, that it is important for the priest to visit the sick and bereaved at the very least, as well as anyone else in need of extra support; this for me is an absolute bare minimum of expectation.

I also worry about the finances of the Church. Many of the churches in the Church of England are old and falling apart and require millions of pounds to sustain them. I worry that the Church's finance model (predominantly financed by the congregation) is an outdated model that relies on the older and wealthier generations. I worry that talk of money actually puts off many younger generations. I believe it has to be something really significant for a family to invest a huge portion of their finances into their church, bearing in mind the current cost of living crisis, with many families struggling to feed their children, and paying for the Church upkeep is the last thing on their minds.

Sadly, from my perspective, the traditional parish church is in sharp decline. I believe there is no single factor causing this, but many reasons over a significant period of time, largely caused by the fact that although it tries, the 'Church model' itself has not changed with the times or at least has not changed quickly enough. On engaging with this problem, I produced the following issues.

First, it is clear that attendance at services has been in decline for many years. Traditionally this has been amongst the younger age brackets (e.g. 20–30), however since Covid there has been an apparent further decline in attendance to services, as people have been given the opportunity to engage through 'Zoom', although this is not itself a bad thing as it allows people who are unable to get to church, or who feel medically vulnerable, to participate.

Secondly, an increasing number of significant revelations over the years with regards to safeguarding have damaged the Christian Church's reputation across the globe. Naturally this has fuelled a lack of trust in the Church, putting people off who may have been curious before, but also driving people away, as they may no longer feel safe or want to be associated with such an institution.

A third factor is a shift in society in general. As the world has become more secular the importance of Sundays has been eroded, and more and more activities, clubs and so forth, take place on a Sunday morning. This means that parents are faced with a choice between bringing their children to church or pursuing a pastime such as sport, where organisers can be ruthless in not allowing children be part of a club if they are not regularly attending. A lack of alternatives such as Saturday night services, means that more pressure is placed on parents to choose between the two.

Fourthly, I do believe that the Church can be inherently sexist, maybe even at times without realising this issue. One of the first comments to me on my first day joining my church six years ago was, 'oh good, a lady, I assume you will not mind joining the flower rota'. If I had not been a committed Christian and keen to be a member of this church, this would have put me off attending again. However, there have been further comments over the years, from both males and females, which show an expectation that women will volunteer for certain jobs due to historic family dynamics when women often did not work outside the home.

Fifthly, I also believe that the Church holds less status these days as it did in the past. It is no longer the community hub that it once was, and the vicars are no longer quite as visible, and therefore as recognisable and respected as leaders in the community as they once were.

Finally, the congregation is ageing, and we have fewer new families attending on a regular basis, mainly because the family model itself has changed. Working patterns mean that parents now spend more time at work compared to thirty to forty years ago. As the cost of living has increased, women have, rightly, been given more status in society. This means that some parents may now be working on Sundays and unable to attend with their children, or simply that Sunday has become a more valuable time for spending with family. Furthermore, with the increased workload of the week, Sunday has become a day where household jobs need to be done.

Editorial Comment: This lay contributor has had a long and active role in the parish system both in the south and north of England. Before she arrived at what she perceived to be the critical issues she made a few points of interest. She admits that there had been problems with the local priest without pinpointing them, but dropping hints as her article unfolded such as poor training. She also observed that in the benefice the local churches 'are different'. There can be problems when different parishes are bound together that have varying styles of worship. A priest nurtured under the evangelical wing of the Church may well find it difficult to lead worship in a 'high' Anglo-Catholic Church, and *vice versa*.

She noted the huge burden placed on retired women, expressed concern that it was critical for the parish priest to visit homes, raised concern about finances with the expectation of support for the Church from families themselves struggling with money problems. She listed what she saw as six critical issues: the decline of the congregation especially among the young, the need for safeguarding because it is a symptom of immoral behaviour, the secularisation of society, the way women are treated, the failure of the parish to be the centre of the community, and the aging congregation.

Many of her points are reflected in this scanning of public opinion, but she also indicates a more singular insight into the damage caused by misbehaviour, emphasised as this is being written, by the resignation of the Archbishop of Canterbury and the developing episcopal catastrophes and contentions often hitting the headlines. She also pointed out that women lay-helpers, despite the fact that women priests are welcomed and widespread, are seen in a diminutive way.

Anonymous

Can They Survive?

This paper is the work of someone who has worshipped for the last forty years or so in a rural parish in North Yorkshire, where he held office at times as a church warden, secretary and PCC chairman as well as serving periodically on the relevant deanery and diocesan synods. The parish was part of a five-church rural benefice officiated for most of his time by a succession of ordained rectors. Neither the parish nor the benefice will be specifically identified by name and when referred to, it will be by the words in italics; both are in the diocese of York. The author was brought up in the Anglican faith and, despite a career which has kept him on the move for most of his life, has generally managed to ascribe to his faith wherever he has been. His observations and commentaries in this paper are purely personal and are not based upon wider research, in depth application to websites or a deep study of the Anglican Church. In short, his observations come from the heart.

Introduction

The Main Issues

Recent years have seen increasing pressure on the Church of England's parish structure with those responsible for leading the Church regularly voicing their concerns as to the future viability of a system which has existed since time immemorial, but it is now showing signs of strain; in some instances, they question the survivability of many individual parishes. Two main reasons exist for these concerns: the willingness of many clergy to serve as parish priests, particularly in rural areas, and the provision of the necessary financial resources to support those priests who do minister to rural congregations which are often themselves poorly financed and geographically widespread; in some rural areas distance can add another disincentive to those seeking to minister at parish level.

The counter argument to the above is that, while recognising that there are real issues about the physical sustainability of the parish system, Parochial Church Councils (PCCs) are determined that the parish system of governance should endure, and ministry be sustained despite the obvious difficulties. As a result, PCCs have generally become grouped into multi-parish benefices to help to ease management problems. Notwithstanding some benefices have now grown so large in numbers of individual parishes as to present new pressures, particularly for their incumbent priests. This short paper is about the arguments which arise and suggest some solutions, although it is accepted that not everybody will necessarily agree with the conclusions. However, those arguments will at least have been aired and may encourage others to add their voices to the debate. Only by giving voice to our concerns and sharing ideas, can we ever hope to bring about beneficial change.

The Parish

The parish in which I live is governed by a PCC of eight people. All contribute according to their abilities and interests. The key offices of secretary, treasurer, organist and church warden are presently all filled, and the Church is well managed. Within an overall plan constructed by the benefice council chaired by the rector, who has similar responsibilities for four other parishes, services are held regularly, although not all of the parishes can have a service every Sunday. Services are led either by the rector or an external, usually retired, local priest or by a lay member of the congregation. At present there are two of the latter in the parish and four in the benefice. Although only permitted to read the prayer book services of morning prayer and evensong, they provide another opportunity to worship and are generally appreciated. Whether the Church at a higher level appreciates their contribution is unknown, but this does seem to be an area where in future, parishes, with diocesan approval, can help themselves at little or no cost. Such services also help to demonstrate to the wider community that a parish is trying to provide the spiritual leadership which is, and always has been, its main purpose. It will however take time for all to accept what may be seen as a revolutionary step, and some training given. If it helps to keep a church in existence and appropriate preparation made, why not? As an afterthought, it is understood that some dioceses have recently instituted training schemes to allow the use of lay worship assistants and lay pastoral assistants. Clearly the sharing of best practice across the Church would be beneficial.

The efficacy of worship at parish level should not be judged purely by how many people attend on a Sunday. While the sophistication of a service and the presence of a celebrant is to be preferred, it is not necessarily everything. Indeed, a service of prayer accompanied by relevant readings and some well-known hymns can often stimulate a congregation and provide an acceptable and enjoyable gathering, particularly in a remote rural area.

Worship by rotating around parishes raises another moot point. Most parishioners are naturally, after centuries of parish level worship, attached to their local church and are often reluctant to travel to worship elsewhere, even though to do so might mean going only a minimal distance. This is disappointing since the rationale underpinning the creation of benefices should also encourage inter-parish harmony. Old habits, aided by ignorance, die hard, but in future if parishes wish to survive, parishioners will need to become more flexible in their approach to where they worship. With goodwill this need not be an insuperable issue. Before leaving the subject of parishes, it needs to be accepted that the key lay officer at parish level is and remains a church warden. Sadly, fewer people seem prepared to take on the role these days, but by definition they are the 'eyes and ears' of a parish priest, and they will become ever more so once 'benefice government' becomes widespread.

Financing a church, its activities and management will always be crucial to its success. A competent treasurer, who may well not be a regular attender or even an adherent of the Christian faith, can reinforce a PCC's confidence if its understanding and expertise results in sensible financial management which, *inter alia,* can boost a PCC's pride in its ability to manage its church's activities.

The Church of England's finance is a complicated subject and one possible reason why there are often few volunteers to be a PCC treasurer. It is widely acknowledged that in York diocese the finance staff are helpful to those who struggle. In this paper it is probably easier to look at finance as a single subject to better understand the role of the diocese, benefice and parish and how they are increasingly linked. That discussion comes later under the heading 'Funding, the Diocese to Parish Link'. Meanwhile at the level of my parish incomings and outgoings, it broadly falls as follows:

Income: in essence comprises planned regular giving, fund raising, service collections, one off bequests, investment income, tax recovery, fees for occasional offices and occasional one-off donations from the benefice or diocese.

Outgoings: these can include building maintenance, electricity/water rates, churchyard upkeep, organ repair, insurance costs, rector's expenses (if appropriate) and annual payments to the diocese (free will offerings, etc.). Also, every fifth-year payment for a quinquennial review, a professional inspection of the Church's fabric. In 2023 this cost the parish £960 which included VAT. This cost is to increase from 2024. Generally speaking, when approached, most people will give their support to help sustain their local church. When there are indications that a PCC may not be able to survive financially this can be met with surprise, mainly because people – whether worshipping parishioners or not – simply do not understand the system by which their church is funded. For them money donated goes to support their church in some mysterious way. They prefer not to be troubled with the details. Indeed, in some instances parishioners may still believe a local landowner has a role in maintaining their church. It must also be said that the statutory annual reporting of a church's audited accounts is not an easily understood exercise.

However, over the years other village institutions once taken for granted, have disappeared, having become unsustainable: schools, shops, pubs, a Post Office and sometimes a library have all come and gone. The one institution which seems permanent and often quite literally indestructible, is the local church which, while it may not be physically well supported, can and does provide a focus for the local community and has often done so in the past. Attendance at a Sunday Eucharist or Matins service should not be seen as the only litmus test of a church's effectiveness and baptisms, weddings, funerals, even confirmation classes, can and do provide a service which people still seem to want although many may not appreciate their relevance until the need arises. Sadly, there is an increasing trend, certainly in relation to funerals, when a parish church is often bypassed with a crematorium service being preferred, for which there are a variety of reasons. However, aware that once lost a parish church may never return, a local community will often rally round when an appeal to raise money for repairs to the Church fabric is launched, while suggestions of a church closure can be met with fierce resistance. In the context of the latter, communities – especially in rural areas – need to accept that, if they consider that their church represents a focus which can draw their community together, they need to give active support to implementing such a role. There are seemingly examples across our nation where this has successfully happened.

Why should such reactions be so? In my experience villages can quickly lose heart if they have no meaningful focus to unite them, and nowadays often only the Church can provide that focus. Of course, village halls can do the same, but they are simply buildings without philosophy or creed. A village without a heart can soon become a soulless dormitory where residents may know or care little about each other and acts of kindness and generosity to one another may rarely occur. The one institution which can reverse such a trend is an active church where an energetic priest who is seen and known, dividing their time with their other parishes, can provide essential *leadership* [writer's emphasis] but they must be supported by lay involvement, namely by committed church wardens. Meanwhile, a priest wearing their dog collar badge of office and walking around a parish can be a welcome sign that the Church is represented in a community.

Reverting to experiences in the parish recent attendance at regular services is showing a slight upward trend; in addition, events of a quasi-religious nature such as concerts and organ recitals and special celebrations at the time of the Church's principal festivals of Christmas, Easter, Harvest or Armistice Sunday have proved popular. These have given the Church a boost and reflect the efforts of the rector and motivated members of the PCC and the congregation resulting in attracting attendance from neighbouring churches. External attendance also means financial contributions so for that reason it is obviously to be encouraged, and if a PCC and their supporters are realistic in what they want to achieve, within reason, anything is possible. Never has it been truer that God helps those who help themselves.

The Benefice

The benefice is at present led by a rector who ministers to five parishes. He joined us two years ago having for family reasons decided to move to the area. He was originally a late entrant to the Church of England having worked in the City of London. On retirement he trained for the ministry and after ordination served as a vicar in a parish in Kent for several years. On retiring following major surgery at the age of 66, he moved to North Yorkshire, considered once again taking a role with the Church but, when diagnosed with a potentially debilitating illness, suspended such plans. On recovery he volunteered to become our benefice rector. As such he receives a half stipend, lives in his own house and works on behalf of his parishioners far beyond his stated hours. He has become well known, respected for his enthusiasm and compassion. His commitment to people is refreshing and widely appreciated and he personifies real leadership.

Prior to the arrival of the present incumbent the benefice had its own priest until 2019 when he left after five years just before Covid. Thereafter the benefice and its parishes were in an interregnum until our suffragan bishop appointed a local trainee for the ministry – termed a focal minister – to oversee the benefice. The impact of Covid and the fact that she was in full-time work while also undergoing ordination training, made her contribution to the benefice difficult, if at times impossible. Meanwhile support from retired priests living locally allowed for the holding of services and occasional offices. Their commitment to helping to maintain worship within the benefice cannot be overstated.

In summary, benefices are here to stay, and those who still consider them only as an administrative stage in the Church's management structure should understand that the current paucity of priests to serve the rural church, precludes the likelihood that every parish will ever again have its own rector. This hard truth must be understood if solutions to the future sustainability of the parish system are to be found. Some years ago, the issue of 'big parishes' was debated in this part of York diocese but, except in one or two cases, went nowhere. The issue which divided people seemed to focus on the position of parish funds: basically, those which had accumulated considerable resources over the years and those which had little residual wealth. How could such positions be resolved? Since at the time the parish took little part in the discussions no further comment is offered, but doubtless the issue will return at some point in the future.

Funding: The Diocese to Parish Link

I do not possess detailed knowledge of the financial systems used to link a diocese with their parishes; indeed, as I understand matters every diocese has its own procedures for financial reporting. This section can therefore only be a layman's overview of how the system works in practice.

At parish level a PCC is responsible for its own costs and income generation. It is not responsible for paying an incumbent but is required to contribute to their costs through an annual free will offering/parish share payment to its diocese; this is interpreted as making as generous a contribution as possible within a parish's overall financial position. In addition, a parish is required to make a range of other payments to its diocese: payments in connection with occasional office services such as weddings or funerals and services taken by outside clergy. Also, a percentage charge can be demanded in respect of a faculty application, for example, for the erection of a headstone or an alteration to a building. Another charge is that levied on a person who wishes to reserve a burial plot, the cost of which is determined by the Diocesan Board of Finance; a recent enquiry to the parish secretary elicited the requirement for the individual in question to pay a fee of just under £600, most of which would accrue to the diocese with there being no certainty that, if the faculty were not granted, only a proportion of the fee would be returned to the applicant.

The system becomes complicated when the role of the benefice is involved since arrangements relevant to the employment of a rector are now understandably conducted principally at that level rather than with individual parishes. A benefice also has its own internal costs of a benefice magazine, fund-raising and any other liabilities which may from time to time be allocated. A grey area from the past is a rectory or vicarage the costs of which now generally falls to the diocese which handles property issues if occupied by a priest, or, if unoccupied, they let the property and take any rent; and decide whether it should be deemed a local rectory or be sold, then the proceeds accrue to the diocese. However, if left empty, the grounds maintenance is the task of the benefice. The issue of who owns a property is sometimes unclear: parish or diocese although York diocese would seem to believe it holds the possession.

The current situation in my benefice is that the rector receives a half-stipend which is currently covered by the combined parish share of the five churches. As a result, parishes in my benefice are net contributors to the diocese, and the rector's position will be reviewed in March 2025. Before the diocese will agree to renewing the rector's half stipend, they will need to be assured that he remains in reasonable health and that the combined parish shares will continue to cover his half stipend. Even so, renewal may be for only two years. Neither housing nor NIS contributions are relevant since the rector occupies his own house and is in receipt of a state pension. This somewhat haphazard way of managing the continued employment of the rector gives no confidence that he will be anything other than a 'stop gap' appointment and that, if the diocese believe that his continued employment may become a financial liability, his tenure could be terminated, and the benefice may once again be placed in an interregnum. The only conclusion to be drawn is that the diocese's financial position is considered more important than trying to maintain a network of ordained clergy across its area.

The Diocese and the Church Beyond

Few people probably fully understand the upper reaches of the Church of England and maybe only if they have been elected members of a synod, and possibly not even then. This can be true of both ordained and lay members of these bodies which exist at every level from deanery to the General Synod itself. Below the latter each of the forty-two dioceses in England has its own synod, dioceses equating in area approximately to English counties and being autonomous in managing their areas. There are approximately 12,500 parishes in England governed by legislation enacted by Parliament, the central church and relevant dioceses. Leaders at diocesan level include the diocesan bishop, one or more suffragan bishops, archdeacons with their own areas to manage and, at deanery level, the lowest level, an area dean and a lay dean.

Sadly, my experience of attending both a diocesan and deanery synod has generally been unfulfilling. Little of consequence was rarely discussed and the general view amongst those attending was sadly of a 'talking shop' where nothing of significance was ever placed on the agenda, nor seemingly intended.

Most contact by diocesan leaders with the laity is through ministry when a sermon encompasses whatever message a preacher intends. In addition, local meetings of diocesan clergy and laity can take place to discuss important issues, or by individual visits to a specific church. In the past archdeacon's 'visitations' to individual parishes have taken place on a regular basis, a good way of communicating, but of late it seems to have lapsed. In discussing the problems of finance and incumbency which are the subject of this paper, the relevant leaders have always appeared sympathetic to the plight of parishes experiencing difficulties, but they have generally seemed unable to offer any real help. Unfortunately, rumours can quickly circulate that the Anglican Church is only really interested in divesting itself of parishes that cannot sustain themselves financially and that, while there are said to be many recruits to the priesthood in training, few seemingly wish to serve the rural Church. Apparently, pressure cannot be applied upon them to do so, if even for only a short period, and clearly an urban parish is always likely to be preferred for its relative ease of management and accessibility.

Rumours also abound as to the Anglican Church's financial position. Little is divulged and the workings of the Church commissioners remains a mystery to most people. Recent suggestions that a large payment should be made by the Anglican Church to atone for a perceived involvement in past slavery practices were received with disbelief, especially when it was said that the Church could easily afford the large sum recommended. At a lower level, recent years have seen a considerable increase in the number of people employed by dioceses; the York diocese website 'who's who' lists over seventy-five individuals employed at headquarters, all of whom presumably require salaries and pension arrangements. Nobody would deny that managing any large organisation in the modern world requires expertise and sound advice, but the esoteric nature of some of the appointments makes people wonder as to their necessity or the contribution they make. No doubt it will be argued that the Church needs the ability to consider and have a view about the great social issues of the day, including those which have caused so much division and unhappiness within its own ranks over the last fifty years, but what is more important: being a 'social service' or 'having a duty for the care of souls through the parish system?' As understood by this author, when a priest is licensed to a parish or benefice, they are given responsibility for the 'cure of souls' (shared with the bishop) and that includes everyone living in a parish or benefice including those who may not necessarily attend church.

While drafting this paper a friend, until recently a non-stipendiary priest, passed me a cutting from a newspaper which, although from some time ago, and therefore probably out of date, makes the very valid point that in many areas the Church has become structurally top heavy. Briefly the cutting stated that in 1901 there were nine suffragan bishops and that (today) there are sixty-five. In 1900, there were 181,000 confirmations; in 1999, there were 37,500. Roughly a 100 per cent increase in numbers of the former and a 79 per cent reduction in the latter. Surely food for thought if the Church's bureaucracy is to be reduced and greater emphasis is to be put on encouraging parish ministry. Of course, this is not a black and white issue, and a sensible balance must be struck between ministry and management with explanations being provided when a diocese feels the need to increase its staffing levels.

Finally, the central training of priests. While this is most definitely not a subject within the competence of the author of this paper, it is, however, an aspect which needs to be mentioned since its success can impinge directly on how well the parish system can operate. Experience at parish level, as in life anywhere, brings contact with all types of people, a rich mixture of talent or not. It is a fact of life that some may be outstanding, some greatly caring but not very stimulating, and sadly, some who should never have been appointed. The priesthood is a vocation, so the above is hardly surprising, but the question must be asked as to whether the Church is seeking the right people to lead at parish level, the frontline of Christianity. Are the rewards, both spiritual and material, for what must be the most demanding job in the Church the right ones? Is the support and leadership given what it should be? Do the rest of us understand what we are asking our priests on the ground to do? These are much wider issues than just at parish level but if we do not get them right then the whole Church will suffer and nowhere more so than in our parishes.

While this is a purely personal thought, but should the parish system eventually collapse, particularly in rural England, would the Church itself be able to survive? After all parishes and their bishops have existed for far longer than many of the transient issues which today so engage the hierarchy and demand the spending of resources. Put another way the Anglican Church is, and always has been, a grass roots movement. Might not the decline of discipleship at the lowest level prove terminal to the whole?

Thoughts For the Future

Some of the thoughts summarised below are drawn from previous sections of this paper, some are ideas already being discussed or implemented across the Church in various places, few are new. There is no wish to re-invent the past, simply to find a way of rejuvenating a centuries old system of faith and worship and preparing it to face the future before it could be too late.

Parishes

- PCCs must accept that the return of a 'one parish one priest' deployment of clergy is unlikely ever to happen again.
- The notion of the parish church as a focus for a community should be re-kindled, there now being few other village institutions in rural areas with the ability to provide such a focus. This can only come from within a church community and will require real *leadership* [writer's emphasis].
- To ensure that services of worship or occasional offices can be regularly held, 'lay service takers' should be given appropriate training and be

licensed to assist their priests when necessary. Inter diocesan best practice training should be widely shared.

- Worshippers must accept that travelling to services within a benefice is not just the best way of utilising scarce Church resources, but also the only way of developing benefice spirit and a greater understanding of what everybody needs to do to help their own parish church to survive.
- In some areas of the country churches have been re-ordered internally so that unused space can be utilised to provide room for a shop or possibly a post office. So long as doing so does not impinge on a church's primary purpose this could be beneficial.
- During interregnums parishes have benefitted enormously from the services of retired clergy who have given unselfishly of their time and experience to minister. However, they may be a diminishing resource, and successors need to be encouraged.
- Pastoral work is at the heart of a parish priest's role in a community. The value of active visiting by a priest needs no emphasis but consideration should be given to developing lay teams to assist and win the confidence of a community.
- Church wardens are the key to maintaining a successful PCC. Their links to their priest are crucial. More attention should be given to encouraging and helping them to be as effective as possible.
- If parishes are to become financially self-sufficient PCCs will need to give more time and effort to having a structured plan for fund raising and to ensure it is followed.
- Involvement by parishioners who may not be regular worshippers but who respect the contribution of their church community, must be harnessed. Greater emphasis upon the wider role a local church can play is vital.
- Those seeking to judge the utility of a particular church should look beyond the register of attendance at services to assess their real impact. Records tell only part of the story.
- A good start to ensuring more proactive leadership at parish level might be to discontinue the term 'PCC' and replace it with a 'St X Church leadership team'.

Benefices

- Benefices are here to stay. Numbers entering ministry alone make it impractical to think otherwise.
- The number of parishes in a benefice needs careful thought. Six is probably the very upper limit but geography needs to be considered carefully. Benefices containing a dozen or more parishes should not be contemplated.
- The system by which parishes and a diocese decide the financing of their priest will in future be handled more and more at benefice level and is already happening in many cases. This is logical and should help to demystify some of the wider Church's financial practices.
- The ongoing debate between the merits and disadvantages of benefices and 'large parishes' needs to be resolved. The ostensible reason for not adopting the latter designation would seem to be founded in the wide disparity of wealth between parishes. This is a nettle waiting to be grasped and the sooner the better.

Dioceses and Above

- The manner in which the Anglican Church has managed itself has changed little in my lifetime. The Archbishops' Council oversees the structure at home and abroad and dioceses manage their areas of responsibility. While most national institutions have undergone considerable change in the last century the Church seems reluctant to do so. Has the time not come for a fundamental management review of how the Church is run and how it communicates with, supports and *leads* its people?
- While the primary role of bishops, archdeacons and those leading at deanery level is to minister to their people, inevitably administrative situations will arise that they may be ill equipped to handle since they lack the necessary training or experience. Men and women of God they may be, but experts in work practices, employment law and human rights is unlikely. Additionally, their workloads probably far exceed what they can realistically achieve in terms of greater dedication to helping their parishes. Again, a review to establish how the Church's

leaders can be most effectively supported in their wide-ranging duties might be useful.

- Money dominates everywhere and no more so than in the Anglican Church. As already mentioned elsewhere, present priorities seem to favour social welfare over assisting parishes to survive. The Church is said to be wealthy. If it is to seriously consider making financial reparations for past errors, then surely more financial aid for less well-off parishes should also be possible? Charity begins at home.
- Whatever may be decided about the way in which the Church is in future organised, the system by which it is financed needs to be as transparent and understood as possible. This may need revision of a system which would appear to operate financially in different ways through forty-two diocesan finance offices.
- The costs of a quinquennial review need to be reviewed. Whether architects or the Church set rates, it seems that prices around £1,000 could be excessive. Maybe a graduated system of charging should be considered?
- Many ordained clergy leave active involvement in the Church at their due retirement date, probably never to minister again. This is their right. Meanwhile, others continue to minister by assisting on a voluntary basis if or when required Permission to Officiate (PTO). They are often glad to keep in touch and to be useful. Might dioceses not maintain central registers of those who would be prepared to be 'on call' to help if required? There are currently said to be around seventy retired priests in York with no known involvement, some of whom might relish the opportunity to undertake a service or even a short placement on an entirely voluntary basis. Such schemes exist in other organisations which recognise the importance of being able to access previous professional skills on a voluntary basis.
- Those graduating as doctors are required by the NHS to serve their first two years where they are needed, rather than where they might wish to practice. Thereafter they can choose to specialise or work in a place of their choice. Might not the same thing be required of those entering the ministry on ordination? Experience gained in this way

could bring benefits later and would help to provide coverage in areas of incumbency shortage, albeit for a short time.
- Central training of candidates for ordination is obviously necessary to ensure the best quality candidates are selected. There should be no short cuts to a future priest's preparation for working in a parish, the most demanding job in the Church.

Last Words

A personal view, as indeed are all the views expressed in this paper, but if the parish system which has been the bedrock upon which the Anglican Church has always rested were to collapse, then the Church itself would probably be weakened to the extent that it too might soon begin to decline. While currently there is seemingly little prospect of a collapse in urban parishes, the reality in rural areas is starker.

One of the sadder aspects of the present situation in the Church's rural parishes is that only a few people appear to be concerned about it. Of course, as with the appointment of the Benefice rector, a suitable individual was eventually selected but not until the bureaucratic processes had been followed in detail; even so the appointment only lasts for two years before review. This is no way to inspire confidence in the management system.

Finally do those at the top of the Church care. Do our leaders and their advisers not understand that the parish system could be in danger of disintegration unless steps are taken to strengthen it? *Leadership* and more professional methods of communication and motivation are required from the very top right down to the most newly appointed church warden. There is little time for delay. Very finally it should be understood that there are a large number of worshippers at parish level, desperate to see change and to have their opinions canvassed, who wish to see change led from the bottom and not just imposed from above.

Editorial Comment: This was a much lengthier reply than expected, but its depth of thought and analysis were in the views of the editors both incisive and critical. As noted in the opening paragraph the contributor has not only had a long experience of the Church of England but came from the top echelons of the British Army, and in retirement became the chairman of an NHS trust, served as deputy leader of North Yorkshire County Council, was a governor and later chairman of a school in York and the author of books on his regiment and on some Anglican cathedrals. He was also a guide at York Minster for ten years. There may be many who may well guess or speculate who he may be, but more importantly is what he had to write. He comes across as a man of deep understanding of organisations including the Church with a love and dedication for the parish system, and his points of view are shared by most. There is little need for further editorial comment as he makes his views crystal clear with supporting evidence and in the last few pages summarises them precisely, and the editorial team are very grateful for this major contribution.

Chapter Four

Letters From Those on the Edge of Parish Life

Introduction

For most people the term 'the fringe' refers to the 'events and shows' that take place on the edge of the Edinburgh Festival. There is another fringe, which is of special interest to members of the Church of England, particularly those of a more traditional turn of mind. This fringe is the large number of people who do not worship in our churches, except for family reasons of baptisms, weddings and funerals, but who nevertheless regard the Church with goodwill or might even regard it as something they belong to.

Take, for example, the man who comes every year to fix up the electrics for the artificial candles in the choir stalls for the carol service but never comes at any other time. Then there is the person who takes their place faithfully on the flower rota, but rarely actually comes to services. Then there is the sort of person who drops off their offspring for children's events at Church, and who is very keen their children attend such things but does not get involved themselves. There are thousands of people in contact with the Church at the time of funerals. Many welcome and indeed expect the Church to be there for them at such times, but they may not become worshippers when it is all over.

Some fringe members do occasionally come to church. They come to carol services and crib services at Christmas and also to services like the all-souls' services or Harvest festivals, but rarely at any other time. There are many people who have this sort of relationship with the Church. They value it and want it here even if it sometimes baffles them.

Some people, especially some clergy, can be very critical of the fringe. They regard its members as half-hearted Christians, people who do not want to commit themselves. Others may think the fringe want it both ways. They want the Church to be there, but do not want to do anything about supporting it in any way. Such attitudes are terribly misguided. The fringe provides a huge pool of potential for the Church. People in it may not respond in the way we would wish, and they may not come to faith when we think they should, but it is not really our business. If we accept that the Church is comprised of those God has called, we need to trust the choices he makes. Also, we should be aware of thinking that the way to salvation that we hope we are following may not be the way for everyone.

Clergy are sometimes puzzled by the spectacle of a regular church attender who has a non-attending partner who, to our eyes at least, is as good, if not a better Christian as regards the life they lead. This is a mystery, but who knows what may happen in God's good time.

Long live the fringe.

Added by Another Editor, The Fringe

As a parish priest, I spend more time with 'the fringe' than I do with those who consider themselves 'committed members' of the Church. They are the young couples who tentatively phone me to discuss the possibility of having a church wedding, who visibly relax when you welcome and encourage them rather than give the rejection they expected. There are the family members experiencing grief at the death of a loved one who truly want to believe there is 'something' to give them hope in their despair, to whom we can show the love and compassion of Christ in its rawest and most powerful way. The fringe includes the new parents who simply know in their hearts that they want their child baptised but cannot easily express why, but to not do so would leave their precious new addition 'lacking' something as they grow up. They are the individuals I meet in various parish contexts who have truly thought about, and questioned, the existence of God and struggle to accept it in purely logical terms yet underneath hold on to that questioning desire to believe. They are my second congregation and, in many ways, my most important congregation for they are the ones on the margins, the ones Christ himself dedicated his time to.

Mike the Plumber

I was, to be frank, astonished when you asked me to write my thoughts on our village parish church, because as you well know I am a real outsider. As you will know, I have been the plumber in this village and surrounding area for some forty years as was my dad before me. Yes, we advertise in the parish magazine, and twice I have repaired the pipes in what you call, I think, the vestry, and each year one of my chaps cleans your gutters out from fallen leaves, but I am not a regular attender. You will recall you buried both my mum and dad many years ago, I was married in the parish church and both my boys, the next generation of plumbers you baptised. Yes, I have come to the occasional carol service and my wife asked me to go with her to a midnight mass. I have to be honest; I am not a convinced believer in the existence of God, though nor am I convinced I am right, I think the term I am looking for is what you once called an agnostic. I remember at my mum's and dad's funerals I desperately wanted to believe and remember leaving the graveyard with a sense of hope in a future beyond where we are now.

In short, I am a user of the Church facilities compared to your normal congregation, but my major thought is that at the moments of joy in our family life at weddings and baptisms we are always welcome, and at moments of stress such as funerals the same applies. I shall never ever forget the time my dad was dying, and the way you came and sat with him holding his hand, when all the medical visitors had stopped coming, but you called by to the very end, and I shall always recall the address you gave at his funeral.

All this makes me think that over the years I have taken the parish church and vicar for granted, and now things are changing in this village. There are no longer regular bus services, the Post Office closed four years ago, the surgery has moved to the next village in some form of amalgamation, and now our local pub has become a restaurant for the wealthier. There was even a move to build on the recreation ground, and many in the village are grateful for the way you and your congregation organised the protest, which encouraged us to think someone could stand up against local bureaucracy.

As I move around our area doing my work as a plumber, I am aware that two churches are closed, and one of my men told me that the closed doors of his local church, which he had hardly entered, felt as if the life and soul of that village had died. I know you now look after three other churches, but last Sunday evening when I had been visiting my old aunty as I drove home, I cannot tell you the sense of pleasure and homeliness I felt when I drove by our church and saw the stained-glass windows glowing from the lights inside. The whole area is my work zone, but this village is my home, and when I saw those lights shining out as I turned the corner, I knew I was home. As an outsider, I feel inadequate to refer to changes in the parish system, and I feel I have no right to express an opinion, except to say the parish church and vicar for me have always been at the centre of local life in a very comfortable way.

Kind regards, Mike.

Editorial Comment: In this letter sent to the local vicar the writer Mike is succinct and to the point. He had used the church for weddings, baptisms, funerals, and appreciated the vicar's pastoral care. Perhaps most interestingly, because of these factors, he sees the parish church as the centre of the community as did one of his workmen in another village when his village church shut down.

Margaret F., Headteacher

Mike the plumber told me that I might have some interest in the parish system you are looking at, because of some views I expressed to him many months ago. I shall be brief because I suspect my views will hold little value. As Mike told you I am not even an Anglican, but when I worship, I tend to go to the Methodist Chapel in the parish. I am the headmistress of the local primary school, which was founded by the Church of England, and surprised I was appointed under these circumstances. That was some twenty years ago, and I retire later this year. There have been three rectors in this parish over my lengthy time here. The first one was elderly but a thorough gentleman who chaired the board meetings. He pulled my leg in the gentlest of fashions when I said I was Methodist inclined in my worship, but he said it was my educational background which was of paramount importance, and he told me he thought the time was not far off when Methodists and Anglicans would unite or should do. He bore no ill well to the sub-chair who was a Roman Catholic priest, and I gathered later they were close friends who played card games or chess every week. He insisted that a cross-section of the parish residents should sit on the board, and when the grocer was invited by the rector to join the board, he told him that he was an atheist, the rector laughed and said he knew, that he would get over it, but the reasons he was being asked was because of his well-known common sense and people respected him and his kindness. When another board member raised the question of the grocer's non-belief, the rector reminded him of the good samaritan who was neither Christian nor Jew but a kind helping alien. This closed that argument, and it was never raised again.

This first rector always took the Monday assembly, and if he could not, I would find another day of the week for him. He had a sense of humour which was always loved by the children, and he told them stories of real-life events and then found a biblical allusion. I shall never forget one when our caretaker appeared in the local press for a speeding fine, and many children and some of the staff 'took the micky' by running by him at speed as if driving. The rector pointed out that Reg, the caretaker, had a reduced fine because he was rushing off to his mother who had been taken seriously ill. He then related the parable of the Pharisee and the publican pointing out to be careful before passing judgment, because that belongs in the final analysis to God.

On another occasion we had a member of staff who upset many children because he was fierce and he was, in his own way of thinking being ironic when telling them off, but it was a more a bitter form of sarcasm, which most of us know can create untold harm. He was a young man and when I talked to the rector, as chairman, about how to handle the situation he suggested a novel approach. This meant that I asked him to attend a training meeting for the staff, some twenty-five of us in the good old days. The rector spoke of his experience of school boards, the importance and influence a teacher can have on the lives of pupils, especially those of the primary school age. He told them the account of the Jesuit claim that give them a child at 7 and they will give you the man, pointing out they 'were on target in their thinking'. He said that when a teacher is interviewed there was one question that they should be asked which would determine whether they should be appointed. I remember the staff being wide awake and leaning forward to hear him. He explained that if a potential staff member had four academic degrees, had many years in teaching, good references, despite all this application strength, this one question had to be answered correctly. I can remember holding my breath wondering what the question would be. He asked, 'is it more important that the children like you, or you like the children?' He gave the answer first rather than embarrass anyone by asking them the question directly. He explained a person should not be in teaching whether it was primary or secondary if they did not like children in the first place. He added that children had a corporate instinct in knowing whether a teacher liked them and would respond accordingly. 'If', he said, 'the children know you like them, their work will improve, their response to you will be better, which means that if you have reason to tell one of them off, it must be seen to be justified and the measure of the telling the pupil off be appropriate, never call them 'kids' as that was meant for goats, and never use force, or even worse', he added, 'avoid sarcasm or mockery'. He managed to get his message home without embarrassing the new member of staff who changed and stayed with us for six years.

A few months after this our caretaker Reg was hit by a steel bolt falling from some scaffolding in town and instantly killed. It was a disaster which had a momentous impact on the school, staff and pupils. The rector already knew Reg's family and when I and many of the staff attended the funeral led by the rector in the parish church, we learnt to our surprise that Reg had been in the army and had dropped by parachute during the Suez Crisis. He talked to the children about Reg and asked them to stand in silence for two minutes in his memory. I have never experienced such a silence with not a moment's slightest shuffling as he managed to show the true qualities of the man always dressed in a blue boiler suit.

On Easters and Christmas festivals, before the school closed, he had the whole school crammed into the church for special services and always explained the nature of the church's worship. He also started a 'Padre's Hour' when on Friday lunchtimes he would make himself available to any individual pupils or groups who wanted a chat or advice. As far as I was concerned, he was a senior member of the staff.

He retired and the Church authorities I gather added another parish to ours, and the new person was pleasant, but did not want to be so involved because the workload had increased. She did call in about once a month but seemed somewhat uncertain about school life and never took an assembly, never wandered into the staff room, and the deputy chairman took the ex-rector's position as chairman. We are now on our third rector during my time in office. He is very young, has a third parish to look after, I wrote to him, but never had a reply and in the last three years I have only seen him once when he took the funeral service of one of my retired staff.

To be totally honest I feel the local church has neglected us. This is not intended as a criticism of the new rectors, but their church load seems to have precluded them from giving the children the time and space. I am told that it took seven months to find the last rector, and the lay people, and especially the old and a retired minister ran the local church with just one service a week. As a non-attender I have no right to pass any other comment, except to add that we miss the local parson's presence of when I first arrived in the village.

I fully understand if you are not interested in my views as an outsider to parish life, but the plumber said you might be curious to hear from me.

Kind regards, Margaret F.

Editorial Comment: This interesting letter came as a total surprise and was mainly due to the plumber Mike talking about his contribution with the local headmistress. She lived in the parish and had experience of three rectors during her time of service, and I gather has now just retired. Her insights have proved interesting by her recalling the differences between the three incumbents in terms of their relationship with the only school in the parish. She was not critical of the two new incumbents which would have been easy for many, but she noted that the increase of the geographical size of their areas of responsibility had caused the issue of church and school losing sight of one another. Children in their own way are the next generation, and it has already been noted that most congregations are elderly. Others have noted that Sunday schools are not as prolific as they once were, and the need to put children at the top of the church's priority list should be essential, and this contributor has underlined this without stating it in some prophetic doom-like fashion. On 7 January, *The Times'* religious affairs correspondent Kaya Burgess, wrote that 'almost a third of the Church of England congregations have zero children aged 16, according to official statistics'. She later added that 'the average Church of England church had 5.1 children in it Sunday congregation, down from 6.3 in 2019'. She quoted Professor Linda Woodhead, head of theology at King's College London, who said 'the Church of England has been in decline and the main reason for this is a failure is of transmission from parents to children. The loss of children is of the utmost significance in predicting further decline.' The lack of religious instruction or knowledge in schools has been commented on, but our thanks go to Margaret for drawing attention to the importance which the parish priest can have in having sound contact in the local schools, and thanks to Mike the plumber for arousing her interest.

Comments by Another Editor: This lady's response certainly gave me pause for thought and brought to mind the question of how priestly ministry is exercised in today's conditions. Her first parish priest was totally dedicated to the local school and even knew the caretaker's family. The second was hardly interested, and the third priest simply steered clear of any commitment. It appears that some clergy have rejected the approach that was considered normal in the past. Many clergy do not see the value of involvement in things which are not directly linked to the Church, or alternatively they feel they do not have time for such matters.

Some critics feel the majority of new priests are evangelicals and have a very different model of how people come to faith, than the model many clergy followed in the past. There may be some truth in this, but there are also other factors.

Many clergy in parishes consider themselves overburdened, mainly because they have to look after many parishes in large, united benefices. This has led to a considerable cultural change among the ranks of the ordained. A quick look at any diocesan website will show how many people are employed in some sort of support role. The notion of 'support' was hardly talked about in the past. The only people they would turn to were archdeacons and bishops, and clergy were expected to get on with their tasks. While this may have been a bit hard on some, is it possible the pendulum has swung too far the other way.

In addition to this, the past clergy were encouraged to make themselves available as much as possible. This could mean being called to the local hospital in the middle of the night. These days clergy are urged to protect their time off and make sure they have adequate holidays. Nowadays it can be quite difficult to contact the local priest at all. Many have their telephones permanently on answerphone, which is not very helpful since the caller does not know their message will be picked up. Using a church website can also be difficult for many. It is often quite hard to find the actual name of the local priest and people are encouraged to use email. It is particularly difficult for funeral directors anxious to arrange a funeral.

What some clergy and some in authority have forgotten is that being a parish priest is the best job in the world. He or she has considerable control over their own timetable and their priorities. There is usually no one telling them what to do or how to do it. Not all the tasks that they undertake are very demanding and many are very enjoyable. This is a huge benefit and something that should be valued. It would be tragic if clergy developed a 'victim' view of themselves.

Life in the parish has certainly changed. Multiple benefices require a new way of working, but we need to make sure our priorities are right. What has always been the strength of Anglican parish ministry is the care of people. Whatever else changes, this must be what we always put first.

Dr K. S., Local GP and Atheist

I am dropping you this note as I have been talking to Mike the plumber about your concerns. You know me of course as I am your doctor and live next door to Mike overlooking the church's graveyard. You will also know from previous conversations that I have no belief and describe myself as an atheist. The only thing which challenged my views was at medical school when I watched surgical operations, and I was stunned by the intricacies of the human body which seemed beyond belief. It remained a problem for me, but human behaviour has kept me an atheist, not least when a member of a church (not your one) tried to seduce my wife. I am very conscious that you have helped in families with which I have had dealings, and I recall the time you persuaded a family to call on me because their son was seriously ill, had they left it another month he would not have survived. Following that occasion, I found you were visiting many of my patients when they were in distress, especially when a person was dying, and your palliative care was probably better than the medical profession could offer, because you offered them hope, almost like a drug for the mind, but that is my atheistic view.

Mike asked me if I would miss the parish church if it closed, which I hope it does not. I recall standing in my bathroom and watching a funeral take place barely a mere 100 yards from where I was shaving. I saw you raise your hand as if you were waving at me, but since then I realise, having watched others and attended a few funerals, you were making the sign of the cross. I recall attending the funeral of that poor girl who died from cancer, a terribly sad occasion, and I had a sense of guilt because as a medical centre we did not react quickly enough. I recall attending a humanist funeral of a medical colleague and coming out of the crematorium feeling depressed, but the way you spoke to that girl's family not only intrigued but impressed me. I tended to see you as a highly professional social worker and care assistant. Your talk of God's love and the concept of the resurrection meant nothing to me, but it worked for the grieving family, which is a form of psychological help needed on such occasions. I have also been invited to attend baptisms and marriages in your church, and the way you talk to people I could see why they value you, as I do, but not your beliefs, but the way you connect with people, which I tend to see as your main job.

I have never, as an atheist, understood the so-called Christian appeal, but was amazed when one morning I rose early to use the facilities and was struck by the fact that through the bathroom blind I thought the church was on fire. It was just getting light but still dark and gloomy. I pulled up the blind and saw you had a bonfire with about thirty to forty people warming yourselves around the heat. How you had encouraged a group of people to join you for a bonfire on the edge of the graveyard before six in the morning bemused me. I saw you in the surgery a few days later about your back pain, and I asked you about these early morning revels, asking if you were passing rum around. You told me, and I had forgotten, that it was Easter Day, and you told me you were all waiting for dawn to greet the risen Christ. That's when we had the discussion on my lack of belief. I am puzzled why an educated and sensible man as you are, can still hold to these medieval myths. I also recall you explaining that you had no problems about me being an atheist, because having told me the story of the good samaritan you then said that we will be judged by what we do to help fellow human beings rather than where we stand in terms of faith. That, I had to say, cheered me up.

I have to confess that when I moved to my house on the edge of the graveyard the church bells felt a nuisance. Clanging away for weddings, tolling for funerals, and the Sunday clarion calls. My wife liked to hear them, and now I confess, during that time they were silent for what I gather was rope repairing, I missed them! I also enjoy those dark evenings when I sit at my desk upstairs and see the stained-glass windows gleaming with the lights inside. I know Mike the plumber feels the same way, and we were grateful to you when you removed the graveyard sign stating, 'No dog walking'. Mike and I often walk our dogs together in the graveyard, often pausing at a grave when one of us recognises a name. Mike is more of an agnostic, but I remain a total atheist. Despite this I hope you stay, not just because I now like church bells, and glowing-coloured windows, but I must say your work in the community is not only good but essential and in a funny sort of way I find difficult to express, the parish church makes for a comfortable community, so hope these difficult times for the Church pass and leave everything as it should be.

Kind regards, Dr K. S.

Editorial Comment: Finding people on the fringe of the parish was considered at first a difficult task. It took one person, Mike the plumber, not only to make his contribution but he then managed to gain an invaluable one from a headteacher, and some remarkable insights from an atheist while strolling together in a dog walk in the parish cemetery. In this contribution from a medical doctor who remains an atheist, his points of view may well reflect that of many others who are conscious of the church building but rarely enter. Both the atheist doctor and the parish priest work for the welfare of the parish residents, and despite differing views obviously respect one another. This contribution demonstrates that even for an ardent atheist the parish and its priest were important. This editor can recall an atheist friend who expressed the view that although he thought the Christian faith was a medieval myth the world was a better place with its teaching of 'love thy neighbour'.

Phone Call to Notes, Johnny

Editor's Comment: This contribution started life as a phone call by a shopkeeper a couple of hundred miles away. His local vicar had mentioned the project which he ignored, then he phoned my study. He explained he was having a change of mind, but he was reluctant to spend time writing out his thoughts, 'I'm good at sums, and I know 2 plus 2 makes 5, otherwise my shop would not make a profit, but I can't spell, and grammar is beyond me'. It was suggested that he could send notes, which he said he would do by post with his wife's help. They came in dribs and drabs with a degree of uncertainty as to which was the final offering. Eventually the contribution was put together, sent back and he confirmed that it reflected what he was trying to say.

Content

His shop had started with his grandparents and his father had continued the work, and on retirement it was taken over by Johnny and his wife and they had kept it going for over twenty-five years. Johnny could recall going to the local church, where he met his wife to be, when they were barely teenagers. The shop started to fail as it was originally a greengrocer's store, and other shops were beginning to open on Sundays with the formidable supermarkets. As a consequence, they bought the butchers next door, then later a newsagent the other side of the butcher, eventually turning it into their own form of local mini supermarket. A major issue was trying not to employ too many staff, which was an ongoing headache. The reason he mentioned this shop-keeping background was that the family felt obliged to open on Sundays and they stopped going to church. It was no problem for Johnny who said he had no faith, was not sure he would like to describe himself as an atheist, but it was no issue for him. He was more concerned about being able to organise brief holidays because they worked a seven-day week from 6.00 am until nearly nine in the evening.

Two years ago, his brother Sam had died in a car accident while on holiday, and he and his wife Anny left the shop in the hands of a trusted employee and attended the funeral at a distant crematorium. It was then he had doubts about whether God existed or not as the funeral was taken by a very pleasant middle-aged woman humanist. This he found had clashed with the way he had felt at his father's funeral five years before. Standing in the ancient parish church he said the service offered a sense of hope that death was not the end of the matter, and the words of hope and undoubted faith by the parish priest had made him feel better, and the edifice of the ancient building gave him a sense of being in God's presence. Whereas in the crematorium it was built like a clinical waiting room, no symbols, no sense of past generations, no feeling of family connections. The humanist offered no hope, just some well-known poems and statements. When they arrived back home, he felt so despondent he went to the parish church with Anny and just sat in a pew in the silence. It was there that he wondered whether he had made 'a life's blunder', as he called it, in not so much by rejecting the Christian faith but by ignoring its ramifications. They were about to leave when standing in the porch the vicar appeared. Johnny only knew him by sight, but Anny had talked to him as a customer. Johnny was surprised the way Anny explained why they had been there, describing the humanist funeral as being 'soul-less'.

Johnny said he found it all rather embarrassing, but the vicar invited them back in and took them to a large round contraption which he called the votive candle-stand. He asked them each to light a small candle in Sam's name, his brother, and to sit in silence for a moment. After about five minutes the vicar said, 'let us pray'. So, Johnny followed Anny, by bowing his head. Johnny could not remember the prayers though they rang bells from his dad's funeral. The vicar prayed that God forgave Sam his various sins we all commit, that he would accept Sam into his loving arms, and that he should rest in the peace of Christ. They left the church with the candles still flickering from the breeze when the door was opened, and Johnny recalled looking back at the candles and felt almost overwhelmed that he had done the right thing, and would always remember the living Sam, not the huge coffin.

He would sometimes take time out from behind the counter to wander to the parish church to light another candle, and he admitted that at times his mind was not on Sam his brother, but where he stood in terms of what he believed, in the way he was living his life, his lack of friendships, and whether there was any truth in a caring God. His life tended to revolve, he concluded, on petty cash from customers whom he only knew by sight and what they usually bought, and most of his life was standing behind a cash till waiting to drop dead from exhaustion. Anny had made arrangements that she was returning to the Sunday morning service, and he was pleasantly surprised when the vicar was buying his cigarettes, which showed he was only human, and he would always ask him 'how he was doing?'

About a year ago he and Anny, mainly through his wife's persuasion, hired a manager they felt they could trust. They did this to have better holidays, stopped working fifteen hours a day, seven days a week, and Johnny attended Sunday morning services. Finally in a short note he confirmed he still had doubts about God, unlike Anny, but somehow when in the Church felt his doubts were wrong, and felt comfortable as he could feel what he described as a 'spiritual presence'. It also provided him with the opportunity of raising his issues of belief with the vicar who was always sympathetic and ready to give him time. His final statement simply stated that 'despite the clinical disposal of his loved brother's remains had, thanks to his visit to the church and the local vicar, had given him hope, and life felt better and somehow more secure'.

Editorial Comment: This contribution came in 'bits and pieces', almost a scrap-paper conversation, and there was a degree of uncertainty about its usefulness until the last moment. It suddenly struck the editor that this workaholic shopkeeper had found a better way of life and a spiritual uplift by seeking comfort in the parish church which, even for a person who was too busy for faith, proved valuable and indicated the importance of 'local' churches, and not taking them for granted.

Chapter Five

Final Observations

Introduction

At this stage it is appropriate to thank those who took the time to write down their views. Some followed suggested guidelines of telling us about their experience and then writing down their views about the parish system. Others wrote letters or sent in notes. Many for a variety of reasons wished to remain anonymous and this has been respected, and in places we assisted by taking out references which could identify them, though there can always be the danger of speculation. Any form of editing was first returned to ensure the contributor was happy with the end result. There was a wide spectrum of people showing a deep interest, from those who were congregational members to a retired army general, from young clergy to a bishop. There were expressed a variety of opinions, and in a few places a clash of opinion, but on the whole as the work drew to a close it was clear that many views were held in common. One of the side features of this project was when contributors spoke of their past experiences, as this more often than not outlined not only the importance of the parish system, but the joy of being part of its life.

However, there are some things the authors of this project need to make clear. First it is *not* a comprehensive study of the Church of England as it is at present. Rather it is an attempt to draw together the views on the parish system by ordinary church people, both ordained and lay, working and retired. Most of the contributions are from people who chose to respond to general appeals, and they were not recruited because they agree about everything or asked to follow a particular line of view, just their honest opinions. The one thing they share is a concern for the future of the parish and a concern that the parish has been marginalised, as the Church of England has become more centralised.

The book is not suggesting that everything is wrong with the Church at present. We recognise many good things are happening, including a better understanding of the nature of the Church with lay people having more opportunities to offer their gifts in the service of Almighty God. The shortage of clergy and the experience of long vacancies has often caused gifted lay people to come forward and do things they were never able to do before. Often, they have discovered new skills and grown in confidence in their faith.

Issues Raised

However, mention of the shortage of clergy raises many issues. Is it something we simply accept or even welcome since it saves the Church money? How has it come about? One of the collects for ember days in The BCP prays for 'the increase of the Sacred Ministry', and this seems a far cry from the passive acceptance by Church leaders that we do not have enough clergy or enough money to pay them. Is there a bit of defeatism here? This was a point raised by both lay people and clergy in many replies. The fact is that interregnums go on and on, during which time the congregational numbers have not improved, and they have decreased. Some mentioned that the vicarage and rectory is often let, or sold, and the money goes to the diocese. It is a curious feature when driving through many areas the number of houses which appear with 'The Ex-Rectory' or 'The Old Vicarage' with one called 'The Gift From Heaven' which, given the sale price, seemed somewhat cynical. The general chatter as to why, tends to revolve around whether it is lack of clergy or money, or a mixture of both. Rarely do the diocese explain, and many are left wondering if the parish will simply be joined to the one next door. In many replies, especially in the section dealing with non-church goers the importance of having one's own local church as an active entity is important to any community, especially in rural areas.

The shortage of clergy has had many ramifications, one noted several times was the short curacy which dominates today's scene. One of the contributors had nearly eight years as a curate, most of the old clergy who were ordained young did two curacies, covering some six years. Today it ranges from less than a year to possibly two years. This is brought about by the shortage of priests and understood, but even the best trained and highly motivated can make mistakes when they are new, which becomes more serious if they are the incumbent or priest in charge. Attached to this issue, which differs from diocese to diocese, is the decrease in post-ordination training which for many retired clergy was seen as essential. We all need time to stop making blunders and mistakes, and good post-ordination training provides a sound navigational map for mind, heart, and soul.

There is some concern about how parish clergy approach their ministry these days. The reduced number of priests means that that it cannot be the same as it was fifty or even twenty-five years ago, but we do not want to lose the good things that were learnt over many years. The Church has for centuries been a pastoral Church, expressing God's love by its simple presence in every community. A common theme is parish visiting, which was the bread and butter of a parish priest's life in years gone by. Some clergy say they have no time for it and in multi-parish benefices it cannot be undertaken in the same way, but surely it is still possible in new ways. The obvious one is for the parish priest to lead a team of volunteers, ideally with some training, but to be available to visit the sick and the dying and any others who might wish to see a priest. This might involve some work in the evenings, since many are at work all day, but many older people are at home, and there are quite a number of people who now work from home. Many parishioners have to work in the evenings.

There is quite a lot in this exploration about the growth of lay ministry in our parishes. Many small village churches are highly dependent on a small number of devoted lay people doing the day-to-day work of the parish. Such parishes may rely on the services of retired, part-time or self-supporting clergy. Such arrangements may work very well, but a constant plea from many such parishes is that 'no one is looking after us'. There is no leader or anyone to bring the whole thing together. Perhaps bishops have tended to think that if the services are being conducted, then the parish is taken care of. This is not the case. What the parish is receiving is cover, not ministry.

Many have expressed dismay at the dramatic growth in the numbers of posts in our diocesan offices, which was constantly mentioned by many who replied. Numbers are not easy to obtain, but it is beyond doubt that these salaried posts have grown greatly. Obviously, the issue of safeguarding is new and requires staff, but a look at a diocesan website Who's Who will show that there are far more people employed than there used to be. A point often made is that the money it costs to employ them would be better spent on staffing the parishes, many of which experience long vacancies. Many, both lay and clergy, have noted the large number of salaries offered, and there were in the replies many criticisms of the reason and value of such appointments. At the basic level it raised the question of money and the way it is raised and spent. When parishes have huge parish quotas, which many feel to be unreasonable, it does not seem unfair that this question is raised. The feeling was expressed that the Church has taken on a business management approach at all levels which some have found not only distasteful but wrong for an organisation based on spiritual values.

In the Church of England there has always been the presence of different traditions. Many would accept that this is one of its strengths, but in recent years the balance has changed. The evangelical wing of the church has become more dominant, and this has had serious implications. This is a difficult and complex issue to reflect on, and it is important to avoid sweeping statements and generalisations, but certain observations are offered here for the reader to think about. Evangelicals are less likely to value traditional ways of doing things, and they tend to put evangelism first and pastoral work second. In practice the two things should never be separated. Good pastoral work is probably the best kind of evangelism. Spirituality takes its own form in the country parishes, and it is not often very ostentatious or obvious, even though it is real. In most towns and cities there are some well attended evangelical/charismatic churches. These certainly serve a need, but they do not provide a model for ministry in most rural parishes or in indeed for most suburban ones. Our past may provide more guidance because many historians have stated that if we do not learn from history, we shall repeat the same mistakes.

Another issue occasionally raised nowadays, is the difficulty of contacting a parish priest. The website A Church Near You provides some information about parishes, but it rarely provides the name of the parish priest. Instead, there is a box where you can 'contact us'. Most people would like to know who they are contacting, before taking the step of making contact and some will specifically want to find a priest and to do so in confidence. Also, many clergy are only contactable by leaving a recorded message, which can be a serious 'put off' for someone in need, or trying to make their first tentative contact with the Church.

All this is a far cry from the time when clergy were encouraged to be as available as possible. Their names were on the church notice boards and on the visiting cards they often used. There are genuine concerns about protecting clergy and their families from unnecessary, unwelcome or nuisance calls, but there must be a balance if they truly seek to serve their parish. Some level of risk has to be accepted, as clergy within the parish system are part of public property for the message of faith and support.

The editors are not professionals in financial matters which is why they sought the help of an expert. One thing often emerged from the replies was the widespread concern of the salaries offered at various diocesan houses for posts, some of which appear to make no sense to many struggling to pay the parish quota. Some may feel that this book is just about looking back. In answer to that charge, it is fair to say the editors are no strangers to change. Someone who was ordained in the 1960s or 1970s will have lived through the introduction of synodical government, the long process of liturgical revision leading to the introduction of common worship, the ordination of women and a lot more, so they are well used to coping with change, and accept that the Church will always be evolving and adapting its way of presenting the eternal message of the Kingdom of God to a changing world. The book is really more an appeal for more vision and more imaginative thinking together with a willingness to learn from the past to keep the message of the Gospel of Christ alive and meaningful.

We know and understand that many of these contributions will not be liked or appreciated by those in top authority and open to all forms of criticism, which is why anonymity was considered so important.

However, it must be recalled, as outlined in the introduction and title, we are only seeking a way the people who work in parishes may have their views, concerns and hopes more widely known. Their main concern boils down to sustaining the parish system, which is the frontline for the Christian faith, which means more clergy and not too large a benefice often deployed to cope with the shortage of priests. If the parish priest has a well-defined area there is more opportunity for visiting and being part of community activity, and both finances and diocesan input is critical. It is known that many dioceses are doing their best, but at ground level many feel that more can and must be done.

Final Editorial Comment: Just when we thought we had finished a website message popped up, written by the Canon Theologian of St Mary's Brecon, Mark Clavier, and it felt right to include his thinking, to which he agreed. See https://open.substack.com/pub/markclavier/p/clergy-burnout-and-the-cure-of-s.

The next few lines are extracts from what he had to write, and they say much. It is entitled *Clergy Burnout and the Cure of Souls*.

When I began ministry in the Church of England sixteen years ago, after serving in the United States, one of my first observations was how stretched our clergy were. This strain showed itself in two significant ways. The more obvious was the relentless cycle of leading worship across multiple parishes while also meeting demands for baptisms, weddings and funerals – what we affectionately call 'hatch, match and dispatch'. For many communities, this remains their primary engagement with the Church, expecting their vicar to be available for life's milestones while otherwise remaining disconnected from parish life. That alone is exhausting work.

But there is a quieter, more insidious weariness. It's the slow erosion of hope that comes from ministering in a landscape of long-term decline. Many clergy spend their entire lives performing the same sacred routines – Sunday services, occasional offices, pastoral visits, civic duties – while the pews grow emptier, the buildings wear down, and the finances dry up. Some serve multiple churches, where the few remaining worshippers barely fill the choir stalls, let alone the sanctuary. The work still holds profound meaning, but the emotional cost is steep.

... If you dig beneath the surface, you find that the roots of this crisis go deeper than declining attendance or administrative overload. What we're really seeing is the gradual loss of something profound – the traditional understanding of the cure of souls. Clergy are ordained to be shepherds not bureaucrats, pastors not managers. Yet increasingly, the modern Church has siphoned their energy towards tasks that pull them away from their true calling: the healing, sustaining, guiding, and reconciling of souls. They've become like doctors so consumed with keeping their clinics open that they've no time to practise medicine.

If we're serious about confronting this crisis, we need to rethink our priorities. The Church needs structures that free clergy to be what they were called to be: pastors and spiritual guides, not institutional caretakers. We must reclaim the rhythms of prayer, sacramental life, and deep engagement with Scripture as central to ministry. Above all, we must remember that clergy aren't mere functionaries, but human beings entrusted with sacred work – work that requires nourishment and renewal just as much as sacrifice and service.

There's a particular kind of loneliness that comes with ministering in a church where decline has become the norm. Many clergy serve in parishes that have been shrinking for decades, where the culture quietly assumes that dwindling numbers are inevitable. I remember attending a clergy gathering some years ago and asking the group if anyone had ever been part of a growing church. The silence that followed was striking. The psychological toll of working under that shadow is profound ... Clergy in these contexts often feel as though they're trying to bail out a sinking ship with a teaspoon. The work remains meaningful, but over time, the slow erosion of hope can wear a person down. Some begin to wonder if they're really called to this work after all. Others simply grow weary, their energy fading like the congregations they serve.

One of the greatest challenges facing clergy today is the sheer weight of responsibility placed upon them, particularly in rural areas. Having ministered in both the US and the UK, I've been struck by how much more demanding ministry is here relative to the size of the congregations. The numbers don't add up. The workload feels relentless.

Imagine being a priest responsible for five, ten, or even fifteen churches. Sundays become logistical feats – a carefully choreographed sprint between parishes for multiple services. Layer on top of that PCC meetings, funerals, school visits, pastoral emergencies, and the myriad unseen responsibilities that clergy are still expected to perform in contexts often entirely unrelated to each other. I once served in a benefice where two villages, though geographically close, were separated by a range of hills and no public transport links. The best will in the world was never going to combine their ministry into one.

The historic parish system – built for a time when each village had its own vicar – is showing its age. Today, shrinking congregations, ageing communities, and diminishing finances have stretched that model to its limits. Each church has its own personality, its own traditions, its own pastoral needs. Clergy crisscross between these communities, never having quite enough time to know any one flock as deeply as they'd like. And because most church goers now don't attend worship on a weekly basis, it can take clergy months just to recognise them, never mind get to know them.

The pressure only intensifies during vacancies. Clergy retire or move on, and those left behind absorb their responsibilities without reinforcements. In some places, one or two priests now conduct the ministry that once required four or five. As a result, urgent needs take precedence, while longer-term spiritual care gets pushed further down the list.

What's lost in all this busy-ness is the heart of the vocation. Many priests find themselves reduced to 'sacramental dispensers' – rushing from one church to another to perform the rituals of baptism, marriage, and burial, without the time to nurture genuine discipleship or provide sustained pastoral care. Many end up functioning more like overworked administrators than shepherds of souls.

As if the demands of multi-parish ministry weren't enough, clergy today are also contending with a rising tide of administrative tasks – many of which feel profoundly disconnected from the heart of their vocation. Safeguarding compliance, property maintenance, financial reporting, risk assessments in multi-church contexts – the to-do list grows ever longer even as the volunteers to help with them grows shorter, transforming priests into reluctant managers rather than spiritual guides.

Even when priests do have neighbouring clergy, the relentless demands of the job leave little time for meaningful fellowship. Each day is a delicate balancing act between pastoral care, liturgical preparation, community obligations, and the ever-growing pile of administrative work. The weight of expectation is constant, and the lack of peer support leaves many clergy feeling like they're carrying it alone.

Too often, clergy are placed in situations where expectations far exceed available resources. They're asked to inspire growth without meaningful support, manage multiple parishes without adequate staffing, and wade through administrative demands that leave little time for pastoral care. The words of Luke 11:46 feel uncomfortably apt: 'You load people with burdens hard to bear, and you yourselves do not lift a finger to ease them'.

We need to rethink how we allocate our resources. No priest should be expected to shepherd a dozen parishes singlehandedly, nor should they be buried under a mountain of administrative tasks that pull them away from the very people they're called to serve. We must streamline these processes and create structures that allow clergy to focus on pastoral and sacramental ministry. Equally, we need to cultivate a culture where support for clergy is not just a sentiment but a lived reality – through genuine opportunities for rest, ongoing formation, and meaningful community.

Most of all, we need to remember why the Church exists. It is not for the mere survival of its institutions but for the proclamation of the Gospel. If we truly believe that, then we cannot allow those called to serve to be left carrying the weight alone, quietly burning out while the rest of us watch. The words of Christ remain as urgent as ever: 'Come to me, all who are weary and burdened, and I will give you rest'. (Matthew 11:28) May we, as a Church, learn to embody that invitation – not only for the sake of our clergy but for the sake of the Gospel itself.

Editorial Comment: It seemed somehow appropriate to conclude with the words of a theologian whom none of us have ever met or knew about.

Editorial Comment: Our lay editor noted there was some 'inhouse' language in the various contributions and he has kindly produced some light on the issue below.

Abbreviations and Glossary

AWA – in the Church of England, an Authorised Worship Assistant (AWA) is a lay person who is formally authorised by a bishop to assist the incumbent (parish priest) with the ministry of the word and in conducting worship within their specific local church context. This authorisation allows them to take the lead in various aspects of worship, including leading services, assisting with the administration of communion, and delivering talks or addresses.

Benefice – a 'benefice office' in the context of the Church of England refers to the administrative hub for a group of churches that are united under a single incumbent (a vicar, rector or priest). It is essentially a central point of contact for all matters related to the united benefice, which may include multiple parishes.

Crockford's Clerical Directory – is the definitive guide to Anglican clergy and churches in the Church of England, the Church of Ireland, the Church of Wales.

Electoral Role – Following the Church Representation Rules every parish church must hold an electoral roll on which are recorded the names of all lay persons worshipping in that church.

HfD, House for Duty – refers to a priest who serves in a non-stipendiary (non-paid) capacity, often in a part-time role, and is provided with accommodation as part of their ministry. This allows them to serve in places where full-time stipendiary posts might not be feasible or unavailable
.

LLM/Reader – in the Church of England, a Licensed Lay Minister (LLM) is a lay person who is licensed by the bishop to serve in a variety of ministerial roles within the Church and beyond. LLMs are theologically trained and equipped to lead worship, preach, conduct pastoral work, and engage in other ministry areas, often serving in collaboration with ordained clergy. They are distinct from ordained ministers, who are called to serve in a specific office, while LLMs bring their unique gifts and skills to the ministry.

Ordinal – a service book, especially used with the form of service used at ordination.

PCC – Parochial Church Council. This is an executive committee of a Church of England parish and consists of clergy and church wardens of the parish, together with representatives of the laity. This body meet to make decisions about the operation of their parish church.

Peak's Commentary on the Bible – is a one-volume (huge) commentary on the Bible, first published in 1919. It also gives special attention to biblical archaeology and the then-recent discoveries of biblical manuscripts.

Priest-in-Charge – in the Church of England, a priest-in-charge is a priest responsible for leading a parish but does not have tenure as an incumbent. This means their appointment is usually for a fixed term or at the pleasure of the bishop, unlike a vicar who holds a more permanent position.

Rector – in the Church of England is the incumbent of a parish where all tithes formerly passed to the incumbent.

STP – Save the Parish. An organisation launched on the 3 August 2021 by a collection of clergy and laity across the Church's theological spectrum to put the parish church at the heart of the Church of England.

Queen Anne's Bounty – was a scheme established in 1704 to financially support poorer clergy in the Church of England. It was a corporation founded by Queen Anne, designed to distribute first fruits and tenths (income from Church of England benefices) to alleviate financial hardship among less well-off clergy members.

UPA – means an 'urban priority area' referring to specific neighbourhoods within a city that are identified as needing particular attention and investment due to factors like high levels of poverty, social challenges, or environmental issues. These areas are often the focus of government programmes, community initiatives, and other efforts aimed at improving living conditions and opportunities.

Vicar – in the Church of England is an incumbent of a parish where tithes formerly passed to a chapter or religious house or to a lay person.